ZEST BOOKS

Connect with Zest!

- zestbooks.net/blog
- zestbooks.net/contests
- twitter.com/zestbooks
- facebook.com/BooksWithATwist

2443 Fillmore Street, Suite 340, San Francisco, CA 94115 | zestbooks.net

Manufactured in Canada | DOC 10 9 8 7 6 5 4 3 2 1

Edited by ERIN MOULTON

THINGS WE HAVEN'T SAID

SEXUAL VIOLENCE SURVIVORS SPEAK OUT

ZEST BOOKS

For those who find their stories here:
You are mighty.
Do. Not. Forget.

TABLE OF CONTENTS

FOREWORD
By SHARON LAMB, EdD, PhD

In the powerful stories that comprise *Things We Haven't Said*, written by individuals who have experienced sexual abuse, exploitation, assault, and violence, the reader is confronted with the paradox of the written word. These survivors "speak out" after, for many, years of silence. Their speaking isn't heard but read. It is quiet and patient, awaiting readers to engage, mull over, and consider at their own pace. Words are tentative, an invitation to a conversation that rarely feels one-sided. The reader enters the world of the writer but can stop reading, skip over parts, skim, or reread. While the reader is separate and in control, if you will, reading provides an experience of deep connection to the writer. But as Erin Moulton, the collector of these pieces, states, reading these stories begins an act of empathy. The choice to read these words is already a choice to empathize.

Erin advises the reader to take care when reading. But in general, I am troubled by the all-too-frequent cry of "triggers" and the appearance of "trigger warnings," which alert people to potentially upsetting content. Often, when we say someone has been *triggered,* this merely indicates that the person is having an emotional response to another person's pain. The individual is reminded of his or her own pain and is, to some extent, revisiting those feelings. But isn't that the basis of empathy?

When the idea of "triggers" was initially brought into conversations about trauma, psychologists worried about PTSD symptoms—such as the uncontrollable reexperiencing of trauma or the extreme reaction of dissociation (blanking out, floating above the body) to cope with potential reexperiencing. But these reactions are rare, much rarer than the typical discomfort a listener or reader may feel while hearing or reading a trauma story. More commonly, we feel sadness, perhaps anger, heartache, and even, maybe, some spacing out as one gets lost in one's own memories and emotions before reconnecting to the storyteller. This seems human to me. Not something we should avoid.

Still, read these stories when you have the space and time to think about them and the people who wrote them. In giving these people our attention and opening ourselves to their experiences, we support the idea that there is no shame in being a victim. Even if these storytellers do not always feel they have risen to the heroic stature of a "survivor," we can relate to them as fellow sufferers.

I want to say a little more about the terms *victim* and *survivor*. Some people who have suffered from abuse or from an assault balk at being called *survivors*, since they do not think their experiences are as bad as others'. While it's true that not all experiences are the same, sometimes this attitude is just a way we cope when something bad befalls us. We focus on, and separate ourselves from, what could have been worse. People also sometimes balk at the word *victim* because it seems to carry so much shame. The word can seem to imply that the individual did nothing to stop what happened, and so perhaps, in doing nothing, was partially responsible. We know now that victims do many things to try to get themselves out of the situations they are in. They find ways to avoid the situation, to fight back, to remove themselves psychologically in the moment, or even to go along with what seems like play. Victims and survivors are always active subjects. Agents. Even when someone awful attempts to turn another person into an object, we maintain our subjectivity as thinking, feeling, reasoning beings. The stories that follow are very clear on this point. Several of the writers warn us not to feel bad for them but for what happened to them. They want us to know that they are not defined by their experience. They are Aster and Stephanie and Dina and Bryson and Misha. They are people who experienced a sexual assault. That's all. Even if that's a lot.

They are survivors and victims with messages of strength for other survivors and victims, messages that defy typical reactions of shame and avoidance. Talk, share, write—that's what they urge. Some found a way to kick, claw, shout, and punch. Some went to court. Others waited and then began to heal. Many of them are deeply connected to art forms: dance, music, and poetry. In reading these pieces, a recurring theme is that the antidote to self-injury is often self-expression through art. And ever present, after each story, is the voice of the patient listener, who substitutes for us, the reader: "Is everything okay now?" Erin reads our minds as we wish fiercely that her contributors will say yes. They rarely do, and yet there is abundant hope at the end of their stories.

In "Hummingbird Hearts" by Carrie Jones, the writer's nana says, "Evil never dies." It does in these pages. It is difficult to say why and how. Yet it does every time a victim or survivor speaks out—and we listen.

———————

Sharon Lamb, EdD, PhD, is a professor of counseling psychology, a therapist, and the author of several books on victimization and healthy sexuality, including The Trouble with Blame, The Secret Lives of Girls, *and* Sex, Therapy, and Kids, *to name a few.*

INTRODUCTION

We were stuffed around the table in the teen space of the public library. Everyone had arrived under the big *READS* mural to put together a script for a movie that we would film and produce over the next eight weeks of summer. I was the teen librarian, in charge of collection development, teen reference, and my favorite, programming. We'd finally reached the busiest time of the year, Summer Read, and our teen movie-making club was a success.

I'd split everyone up into small groups to brainstorm ideas. Then, like I often do with groups, I milled around and listened, lending a hand and moderating as needed. All sorts of ideas were raised, from haunted libraries to ransom notes to supervillain stories. I'd successfully redirected one group that went off course with an animation idea, and then I heard one word from the other side of the table.

Rape.

I looked over to see two boys laughing while another one looked away. Were they plotting a story? Telling a joke? All I'd heard was the end of it, but that one word rang like a bell above the rest. The only girl in that group had not missed it, either. She was new, from a few towns away. Her green hair swirled into a ponytail, and a pair of purple glasses accented her face. She hadn't said much since arriving, and though she didn't look up, she did speak now.

"Hey, some of us have bad memories," she said, as I navigated my way over. The boy who had said it grew quiet. Papers ruffled, pens started scribbling. They saw me coming, so maybe they thought they were in trouble, or perhaps the quiet was a sudden detection of discomfort. I know I was uncomfortable. I wanted to spend the hour brainstorming silly ideas, not addressing the seriousness of rape with teens.

As I got to their corner, I asked if everything was all right, and they quickly agreed. The girl didn't appeal to me for help. Instead, she picked at the edge of her spiral notebook and fidgeted her feet. Moments later, the quiet boy broke the silence, and the group returned to brainstorming movie ideas.

I found I was equally eager to move on. After all, I hadn't heard the entire exchange. I found myself saying one of those annoying adult phrases that I'd heard over and over as a teen.

"Let's stay on task."

Seriously. *Let's stay on task.* How diminishing. How unhelpful. How cowardly.

That moment stayed with me all summer as I learned more about the girl. She was in foster care, and things had "turned around," she said. She never openly shared with me exactly what had turned around, but she made it apparent that she had a certain set of bad memories. I wondered whether she had been raped. If that was the case, how uncomfortable must that joke have made her? How uninviting to have those bad memories stirred up in the middle of a teen club, in a new place?

I replayed the situation in my mind and realized how unprepared I'd been to discuss sexual violence. What was I supposed to say? It's something we almost never talk about—not in our families, our schools, or our society. Some of us use words related to sexual violence—words like *rape, incest, sexual assault,* and *pedophilia*—with too much lightness. Some of us cringe at any reference to them. We've become better at discussing sexual assault on college campuses, but when the conversation shifts to children and teens, I find we don't know how to talk about it. Not really.

Later that year, I was tasked with weeding the teen nonfiction titles. Weeding is a process where you pull outdated or worn materials and refresh your collection. I was working through the 300s (the social sciences) and came to resources on rape. We had a number of good texts for adults, but the same couldn't be said for the teen collection.

I scrolled through my mental card catalog and a number of reputable fiction titles came to mind: *Speak* by Laurie Halse Anderson, *Forgive Me, Leonard Peacock* by Matthew Quick, *The Perks of Being a Wallflower* by Stephen Chbosky, and *Exit, Pursued by a Bear* by E. K. Johnston. Though formidable and moving, these books are not dedicated to providing information and guidance. They are fictional stories rather than practical resources. Nonfiction pickings were slim. I found a book about knowing your rights as a teenager, which included some information on assault. I also found an outdated title that featured a cover showing a kid with a hand over her mouth. It hadn't been taken out since the year 2000. *Not surprising,* I remember thinking. I extended my search to collections outside of our library to a similar result.

This lack of teen resources on sexual violence got me pondering what kind of book I would want on this topic. What would such a book look like for teens? First, I would want this work to speak to those who have "bad memories" as well as to those who don't, but who want help navigating and understanding the topic of sexual violence. I thought a good format might be an anthology, one in the spirit of *Dear Bully* and *Dear Teen Me*. This anthology would present stories of hope from adults who have survived rape, incest, sexual abuse, and sexual assault as children and adolescents. Done right, I thought such a book could accomplish a few important goals: It could make significant connections to readers who have endured or are enduring similar trauma. It could give valuable perspective on these experiences to "outsiders," to those who haven't suffered abuse. It could include and encourage conversations about the societal issues related to sexual violence. And it could provide concrete information, such as statistics on sexual violence, defining terms, where to find help, and more.

Of course, it occurred to me that, if I felt so strongly that we needed such a book, perhaps I needed to be the one to create it. But was I equipped to champion this project? I wasn't sure that I was the right person for the job, mostly because I am not myself a survivor of sexual violence. However, I am a helper, a teen advocate, and a writer, and as an author, I have some experience discussing a stigmatized topic. While I was working on my book *Chasing the Milky Way*—a middle-grade contemporary novel about robots, best friends, and bipolar disorder—I delved into the idea of bibliotherapy. While writing an article for *School Library Journal* ("Bibliotherapy for Teens," 2014), I spoke with counselors about the experience of reading and how books can be effective in showing teens that their experiences are not isolated. Anecdotally, books can even teach coping strategies through the narrative process. Seeing a character come through a difficult experience or time period can provide teen readers with insight and hope for the future. For a reader who is outside of the situation depicted in the book, the process of reading can also provide an avenue to empathy.

Naturally, as a children's author and a part-time librarian, I am a big fan of books. I like the pace and solitude of them. Books allow you to connect and formulate ideas and opinions without the fury of online comments or the unwelcome presence of trolls. A book contains a world inside itself, a conversation happening on the page just begging to be considered and discussed elsewhere. Books are reliable and dependable. They wait patiently, not going anywhere, until the reader is ready.

Once I worked up my courage to create this book, I had to figure out what the format should be. I wanted both information and storytelling. I wanted engaging writing, and I wanted contributors to tell their stories in their own ways. Like fiction, these narratives and essays would help readers understand and grapple with the complexity of the topic. Yet, I also wanted contributors to talk directly to readers, so the book felt like a conversation that provided guidance and advice. Ultimately, I settled on what you have in your hands, an anthology with a twist.

Here is what you'll find:

- *Creative and Narrative Nonfiction:* Each contributor has written a piece of creative nonfiction specifically for this anthology. Creative writing engages our brain differently than informational text. Through form, imagery, sensory details, and language, creative writing helps us focus and empathize from a safe distance: an armchair, a desk, a park bench. These pieces take the form of poetry, short stories, essays, vignettes, imagined letters, diary entries, and more. Each writer decided what to say and how: Some focused on the abuse itself, some on later years; some emphasized suffering, and some reclamation. Each writer also decided whether to use real names or pseudonyms within his or her piece.

- *Unfiltered Conversations:* Following each person's creative piece is, in essence, a conversation. As a reader, I had questions about each person's experience, and so I asked them about what happened then and who they are now. I call these sections "unfiltered" because each survivor answered in his or her own way. Some answers are the span of a tweet; some are lengthy. Some exchanges were conducted over email; some were conducted by phone while the interviewee was driving across state lines. Some were formal, some informal. These conversations have been edited lightly for punctuation and grammar, and sometimes for length, but the aim is not art or polish but authenticity—frank and open conversations about personal journeys and society today. Beyond discussions of recovery and hope, I wanted to discuss current important topics, such as rape culture, trigger warnings, victim blaming, and more. Of course, these conversations don't provide hard-and-fast answers, but hopefully they provide informed perspectives that can be a springboard for even more conversation.

- *Concrete Information:* Lastly, especially in the backmatter, this book provides further information on terms and definitions, current statistics on sexual violence in US society, a list of hotlines and further resources, and a bibliography of good fiction and nonfiction books.

Once I had the framework, I needed an army of brave anthologists to share their stories. Who are the people you will meet in this book, and how did I find them? When I first started looking for contributors, I approached a few authors I knew who had spoken about their experiences online or by writing books. However, I quickly realized that approaching people unasked could spark strong positive and negative reactions. I was immediately regretful of the people who felt hurt by my request, since my intentions were not to stir up bad memories for anyone. So I changed my approach: I sent out general queries with submission guidelines to various survivor advocacy groups, and I let people who wanted to be involved reach out to me on their terms.

Stories slowly trickled in. When I asked people why they were interested in the project, more often than not, they said they were sick of the silence.

As Jane stated: "I want to be the voice I was looking for as a teenager."

Initially, most of the stories I received were from Caucasian women, and so I sent out another query specifying my need for a diverse group of voices. I wanted this anthology to include stories that represent a wide variety of races, genders, sexual orientations, ages, career paths, and survival experiences. Steadily, the anthology grew and grew, until it became this well-rounded collection.

In these pages, you will hear from twenty-five honest, outspoken, and fearless people. Each experienced rape, sexual assault, abuse, or exploitation between the ages of four and nineteen—or between preschool and the first year of college. These writers share deeply personal aspects of their lives, experiences, and emotions. These men and women come from all walks of life: They include truck drivers, competitive picklers, aspiring chemists, travelers, writers, authors, stay-at-home parents, advocates, artists, academics, and workers. Some are abled, and some are differently abled. They are straight, gay, bisexual. They include Caucasian Americans, African Americans, Native Alaskans, and Asian Americans. Some grew up in the 1970s, and some grew up in the 2000s. And so much more. You'll get to know each survivor in their own words from their personal bios at the end of each piece.

Nevertheless, it's important to recognize that, while I've made every effort to represent a multitude of people and experiences, this is not an exhaustive list. These stories do not represent every type of person nor every type of sexual violence. This book does not include everything there is to say. Rather than provide all the answers, this book is meant to start conversations, since each person's experience of sexual violence will be different, and each person's reaction and recovery will be different. There is no universal truth about sexual violence, nor, unfortunately, is there a universal remedy.

And yet, as I put this book together, a few throughlines emerged, and I'd like to share these with you now.

First of all, *the majority of perpetrators were known to the victims.* We often think of rape as something done by a violent stranger in the dark of the night. But this is a rape myth and not a reality. National statistics bear this out. Several studies have shown that perhaps three-quarters of sexual violence involves an offender who is a family member, intimate partner, friend, or acquaintance (for statistics on sexual violence, see page 193). In this book, Aster, Laura, Shanyn, and Ella were abused by their fathers. Maya's perpetrator was "the cousin from hell"; Carrie was assaulted by Uncle Al. Meanwhile, Allison knew the guy from school, and Stephanie was raped by neighborhood boys, and on and on. All of these stories clearly show that rape happens within communities, at home, and in

Second, *many survivors said they had no language to define the incident.* In other words, as children, the survivors didn't have the words or understandings to identify what had happened as rape, incest, abuse, or assault. Of course, as we develop, we learn words in our homes, schools, and communities. But if abuse is normalized at home, and the subject is stigmatized in society, then how will a child know that she or he is being, or has been, abused? Knowledge is power. Communication is power. Words are power. This is why I felt it was vital to include a "dictionary" of terms and definitions in this book (see page 197). Defining sexual violence is more difficult than you might think, since each state has different legal definitions for what constitutes consent, assault, rape, and incest. But variations of the law aside, becoming familiar with this language is essential. If you can learn these words, you can wield them.

Third, *many survivors were disempowered by more than just the perpetrator.* In almost every story, survivors describe being disempowered not only by the perpetrator but by others as well. For Dina and Shanyn, it was when they spoke to a trusted adult and weren't believed. For Joan, it was when she was told she was asking for it. For Larena, it was when she passed a graphic note in class, and instead of investigating further, the teacher handed the note straight to her abuser, her stepfather. For Stephanie, it was when she reported to the police, and she was interrogated as if she had committed the crime. For Don, it was when the court decided it was too stressful for him to continue testimony. People in power can oftentimes fail the victims. They can be disbelieving adults, poor peer allies, biased police officers, and apathetic teachers. These people may miss speaking up or even listening when given a chance, or they may even send the person straight back into the perpetrator's hands.

And yet, for the contributors in this book, their power is back.

Here, they speak. Here, we listen. Perhaps the act of listening can be as empowering as the act of speaking. Perhaps the act of reading can be as empowering as the act of writing. I believe this to be true. Maybe reading these stories will give you a level of understanding that you didn't have before and motivate you to create change. Small changes, big changes—they all have impact.

create change. Small changes, big changes—they all have impact. Maybe you will read this and be motivated to further explore terms for a class presentation on "victim blaming" and "rape culture." Maybe reading this will inspire you to explore books on happiness and healing—or better yet, to start a sexual violence awareness book club (for book ideas, see Recommended Reading, page 204). Maybe reading this will help you become a better ally or a victim's advocate. Maybe reading this will inspire you to petition your educational system to discuss juvenile sexual violence (if the education at your school is lacking). Maybe reading this will prompt you to work with your community or police department to provide quality resources for victims.

Most of all, I hope you read this and find the power of your own voice.

I hope that you are inspired to speak out when you can. To stop that rape joke. To be an ally to the kid with bad memories. Instead of changing the subject, fill the uncomfortable silence with an unwavering voice. I know I will.

And, reader, if you find a story in this book that is similar to your story, I hope it brings you some comfort in knowing that you are not alone. That things get better. That there are coping mechanisms and resources. But most of all—that your voice is irreplaceable, irrepressible, brilliant, and mighty.

Do not forget.

Finally, take care and time reading this content. It's been my honor to edit this book and my honor to get to know these survivors. Now it's your turn.

Best Wishes,
Erin E. Moulton

Erin E. Moulton is the author of Flutter *(Penguin, 2011),* Tracing Stars *(Penguin, 2012),* Chasing the Milky Way *(Penguin, 2014), and* Keepers of the Labyrinth *(Penguin, 2015). Her books have been selected and nominated for national and state award lists, such as the Amelia Bloomer List, the Kentucky Bluegrass Award Master List, and the Isinglass Teen Read Award List.* Flutter *was also a 2011 Kid's Indie Next pick. Erin works as a teen librarian at the public library where she maintains a collection of awesome YA books and leads teen programming. Erin loves fostering new voices, which makes her an active school visitor, mentor, and workshop leader to writers of all ages. You can find her online at www.erinemoulton.com.*

THEIR STORIES

YOUR VOICE
By ELLA ANDREWS

I loved words as a child,
kept lists, devoured books,
read the ingredients on the Cornflakes box,
spelled them out,
rolled them around my mouth.
They had texture, taste.
I pored over treasured books through glasses
too big for my freckled face.
I kept vocabulary lists.
I still do.
Finding an unfamiliar term,
like discovering a secret about an old friend.
Language becomes new again.
And yet I had no words to explain
what happened at night
in my father's bed.
My doll, tucked safely in the blanket-cocoon
I made for her,
was mute.
And so was I.
I was a "good girl," "daddy's little helper."
He said "jump,"
and I asked how high.
"Smart as a whip," "she'll go far."

I went inward.

I took the unformed words,
the unuttered cries for help,
and withdrew into myself.

I learned the words later
but stammer over them still.
Sex ... abuse ... rape,
and ... worst of all
incest
which I can never say.
The words seep out slowly,
sometimes,
as I whisper my fears
to someone I hope—one day—to trust.
Or in sobs, as I retch out the
pain and shame,
the humiliation which wrapped itself around my bones
and grew with me.
I don't know when it will end,
when the words will finally live outside me.

But now I have you, my beautiful miniature.
At nine months old you have a library larger than most adults.
I teach you words, point things out,
feed you language with your pureed peas,
relish the moment when you say your first word
and we dance around the room
gleefully shouting out "cat" again and again.
Soon words are pouring out.
I watch you, in your crib, talking to your stuffed toys.
Then your favorite word is "no" and you repeat it often
And loudly.

When I load your backpack with pencils,
your lunchbox with love notes
and send you to school
your teachers complain that you talk through class.
I tell them we will work on it
but I smile,
I'm quietly proud—your words won't be contained.

You start to write.
First the alphabet, then your name.
Soon you are writing letters to Santa,
lists of toys you can't live without.

Then come stories, poems, and essays.
You join the debate club.
Words flow easily for you.
They seem to have a melody
and you, the composer,
stand tall.

Too soon there will be college applications,
and I know I'll have to listen to your words
through the other end of a telephone.

But this I know.
When you pack your things
and we try to cram an entire dorm room into the sedan
you'll take with you the knowledge that,
for you, no words are off-limits, too scary to utter.
No secrets to keep locked away
shards of letters to torture you from within,
and no matter what you say
I Will Always Love Your *Voice.*

ELLA UNFILTERED

WORDS AND REFUGE

Ella, thank you for this powerful poem, which is all about speaking and finding your voice. Let's talk about voice for a minute. Who was the first person you told about your experience?
My therapist. It took me two years to trust her enough to tell her, and even then, I was terrified that saying the words out loud would make

it real, that she would be disgusted or blame me, that she wouldn't believe me, that she *would* believe me—when I didn't want to believe it myself—that she would push me to reveal more than I was willing, and so on. At its root, I was scared of no longer having control over this secret. Yes, she really heard me, and I felt a strange mixture of fear at having to confront this and relief that I wouldn't have to do it alone. When I told her, I immediately wanted to run away and hide. I felt so vulnerable and raw disclosing the things I've kept hidden for so long. But she has been consistently supportive and encouraging, and she lets me go at my own pace, even if that pace seems incredibly slow to me!

You grew up in this situation. Did you know you were being sexually abused?
No, I was too young. I knew I was uncomfortable with it. I knew I wasn't supposed to tell anyone. I felt that something very wrong was happening, but I assumed that my feelings were wrong and my abuser was right. He was the adult, and my father, so I reasoned that he couldn't be doing something harmful to me. I don't think I fully realized that I had been abused until I told someone. As I was saying the words—hoping my therapist would say that I was making too big a deal of it or that I must be mistaken—I knew she wouldn't. I *knew* what had happened to me was wrong. Saying it made me realize that I had always known it.

How is recovery going? Do you feel that you are recovered?
No, I don't think I have fully recovered. "Recovering" implies going back to a pre-abuse state, and I'm not sure that's possible for me, since I was so young when it started. The abuse affected many aspects of my development—emotional, physical, spiritual, and sexual. As I told my therapist, I think I'm still, in large part, surveying the damage. However, I do think I am "becoming" and "discovering" my new self. I will never be the person I would have been if I had grown up without the abuse, but I am excited to find out about the new person I am becoming. I am learning to separate what happened to me with who I am. I like myself and trust my inner self more now than I ever have, and I think that will continue to grow as I keep working through what happened to me.

As a kid, was there a certain coping mechanism that worked for you?
For me it was reading and writing. Reading fiction was an escape
during the years in which I was abused—I could go somewhere else
in my mind. I felt safe in my books. I don't remember a time when
I didn't read and write prolifically. There were so many things I
couldn't say to my abuser, to my family and friends, to my teachers,
but I could pour my thoughts onto the pages of a journal and that
made it so much more bearable. I started to write poetry when I was
eight. I found joy in creating something structured out of thoughts
that seemed chaotic. I also found poetry deeply beautiful. Creating
poems which I find both truthful and beautiful reminds me that
there is beauty inside me that nothing which was done to me could
ever touch.

*You loved words as a child, and you use them very well as an adult. Is
there a particular title that was a favorite? Or one that you found at just
the right time?*
I was a fairly precocious child and loved nineteenth-century novels.
I was obsessed with the Brontë sisters—I loved the idea of three
sisters (and their brother) living and creating masterful novels
close to the wild moors. Their description of nature—especially
in *Wuthering Heights*—really drew me in. I, too, loved the wildness
of nature—especially a stormy sea with a ferocious salty wind
blasting against my face and blowing through my hair. It made me
feel elemental and completely free. I was also fascinated by their
juvenilia—the idea that children could create a fantastic world for
themselves. A world where they are in control. I often felt powerless
as a child, and this inspired me to write—to create my own order, to
explore a character or an idea. Writing was also a bit subversive for
me. My parents knew that I wrote poetry and would often ask me to
write poems for birthday cards and special occasions, so I became
adept at a greetings-card kind of poetry. But the real stuff—the
writing in which I could create my own order, explore a character or
an idea—that I kept as my refuge. No one could take it away.

What would you like to say to a teen or kid in your situation?
Trust yourself. You have a deep inner wisdom. If you think
something that happened to you was wrong, trust that feeling. I

would also like to say that you have the potential within you for great healing. Despite what has happened to you, you're here—you got through it, you're getting through it every day, you're strong. You may need help to access the healing within yourself—I did—and there are many people who can do that, but you have it within yourself to heal.

ELLA TODAY

Ella Andrews lives in Boston with her wife, son, frenetic dog, and a cat who keeps them all in line. She works in university administration helping students to make the most of their time at college. She also reads and writes poetry.

LETTER TO THE DEACON
By DINA BLACK

Dear Deacon,

When I was a young girl, I trusted the world and everybody in it. I believed that people were honest. I believed that people where loving, caring, and compassionate and that they didn't intentionally hurt one another—not physically nor with lies.

In Ohio, where I grew up, we came from the suburbs. We could ride our bikes until dark. We would ride from one side of town to another. We would hang out with our friends well into the night, on the front porch, or play kickball by the street lights. We could even leave our bikes out all night long and no one would think to take them. Many nights, we slept on our back porch or with our back doors unlocked, and we were never afraid. I always felt safe. Most of the people I was surrounded by went to church every Sunday, Wednesday, and Friday. As you know, my grandfather was the founder of the church, and my grandmother was the first lady of the church. I loved walking around the church, seeing many photographs of my grandfather preaching and teaching and helping those in need. I was so proud that many of the members of the church, in some way or another, were related to me.

I had no reason to doubt anyone's goodness.

But then there was you.

One day, I remember, I had to go to the bathroom, which was located in the basement of the church. Down in the basement were seven Sunday school classrooms, the baptismal pool, and the supply closet. We all had spent so much time in the basement that we knew every inch. We used to play hide and seek down there while our parents where in choir rehearsal, so there was no need to be afraid to go to the bathroom. Even all the adults had no problem sending a child to the basement to go to the restroom or even to get something out of the supply closet. It wasn't even spooky.

But that day, you were in the basement, and that day, you waited until I came out of the bathroom.

You said to me, "Dina, come here for a minute."

You were down the hall in one of the Sunday school rooms, and I came as you asked, and I remember you just talked to me about how I was doing, and then you asked if I was going to the candy store after church, which was what most of the kids did when we had money to do so. I said no. I didn't have any money for that. The money I had, my mother told me to put in church. You reached in your pocket and gave me fifty cents. To a six-year-old, it might as well have been a hundred dollars.

You told me that I couldn't tell anyone because then they would want you to give them money as well. You told me it was only for me. You patted me on my butt and sent me back upstairs with fifty cents. A secret and a pat on the butt was the beginning of your manipulation. This went on for several weeks. Then I started looking for you so that I would get my fifty cents.

Then you went from a pat on the butt to sitting me on your lap, to rubbing my butt, to putting your hands up my dress. You went from fifty cents to a dollar. You raised the amount because I got scared, and you assured me there was nothing to be afraid of.

You were smart. You took your time, and you trained me to respond to you the way you needed. It was not like a rapist who just snatches a person, commits the act, and then moves on. No. You manipulated the situation and groomed me until, one day, I was no longer afraid. I was guilty.

Guilty for letting this happen and not saying anything.

Guilty for taking the money and buying candy.

Guilty for liking the way it felt.

Guilty for not telling someone when I knew it was wrong.

So things continued to escalate over the years, until, eventually, I didn't feel afraid. I didn't feel guilty. I didn't feel hurt. I felt numb and ashamed. That shame sent me to a closet. That shame put me in a place where I could not tell anyone. You recognized that I was there, and you graduated to doing more touching, feeling, making me touch you, and you penetrating me.

And after that, I really couldn't tell.

You changed my world. You shattered everything I was ever taught about love and protection, authority and, most of all, people of the church. What made you, as a grown man, think that it was okay to touch a six-year-old child in ways that you would only touch another consenting adult? What made you think that it was okay to turn on the sexual drive or desire of a baby? What was wrong in your heart and mind that would cause you to go through such a heinous act and forever change the course of my life? You not only did this once, but you did this to me for years.

You made me change how I saw the world and how I saw myself. I began to feel that something was wrong with me because I went from being afraid of you—and what you were doing to me—to wanting it, in some strange way, because it felt good. It awoke sexual feelings that I was too young to understand or know how to deal with. It made me more afraid to tell because I felt I caused it.

My heart was hurt, and my head was messed up.

It took me going through counseling to understand that none of this was my fault. You owned every bit of it, and I have been stuck with the repercussions. It was you who caused me to be afraid of my own shadow. I had believed for years that there was something so wrong with me—that I was not worthy of good healthy relationships with people. As a matter of fact, I had no idea what a healthy relationship looked like. I have spent time being confused about my sexuality.

Wait, I had been taught. I had been taught how precious and sacred my sexuality was, and how I was supposed to abstain until marriage. I never got the chance to feel it was precious or special because of you.

You perverted my sexuality.

You perverted my understanding.

You perverted my character.

You violated me at the core of my being.

You abused the very seat you sat in.

I have come to understand, years later, that I was not your only victim. All of the stories, according to my aunt, are similar in nature. You gained their trust, offered something they wanted, and you manipulated them over time to do what you wanted without them ever saying a word. A story that I know all too well. The funny thing is that I don't know which of the family members this was done to because my aunt was a confidante for most of us, and she never revealed any of the names, but we have become aware that we were not your only victims.

Speaking of family, I spent a lot of time angry with my grandmother, not outwardly, but in my heart, because you were her brother. When I tried to tell her, she shushed me. I know you must remember the day you thought the gig was up. After church one Sunday, we did like we had always done for many years, went over to my grandmother's after church to have dinner.

On this day, I had decided this was the last day for this behavior. I would tell on you, and you would go to jail.

I remember saying, "Grandma, I need to tell you something."

"What child? What do you want?"

I said, "Grandma, Uncle has been touching me in my private parts."

I remember she looked at you and said, "What? You did what?"

You said, "I smacked her on the butt for running down the stairs."

"No, Grandma. That's not true. He touched me in my private parts."

My grandmother said to me, "Child, go somewhere and play, and stop running through the church."

"But he is lying."

She got really upset at me for calling you a liar and told me to get out of the room. Grown folks were talking and I knew better than to be so disrespectful. I started crying and screaming and slamming things, and that just upset her till she was adamant about me leaving the room and stopping all that lying. I was destroyed. You won.

The day she silenced me, and accused me of being disrespectful in front of you, she gave you the power to continue to hurt me and to add others to your list.

I became bitter. Bitterness caused me to come very close to destroying my life.

I remember when I was in junior high and high school, I played a lot of dangerous games. While in junior high I started going out with guys who were abusive, or I would be looking to get something out of these guys without having to give up anything. I was trying to manipulate guys, and I came very close on several occasions to getting myself killed because I did not know what I was doing. I just wanted to do what had been done to me: manipulate someone to get what I wanted. I didn't even know what it was that I wanted except to feel control over someone.

In high school, I started dating guys, and some I was sexually promiscuous with, and others I would act as if I was still a virgin. I felt bipolar. I dated guys who meant me no good. And those that cared about me? I meant them no good. I started drinking and doing drugs, not realizing that I was doing that to escape my negative self-image.

The funny thing is, everyone who knew me thought I was bold, confident, smart, and kind. No one knew I felt I was dying on the inside. I felt I could never and would never find love, and yet I was afraid of finding love because that meant I would have to be vulnerable to someone else, and I couldn't do that because then they would only take advantage of me. Well, that had been my story, thanks to you.

You have caused me years of hurt and pain. I wasted a lot of time hating you and being bitter after what you did to me. I am thankful for counseling and for people praying for me. They helped me to understand that I didn't have a problem. You had a problem, but because it was hard for me to get help early in the process, I spent too much time in such negative space that was only painful to me. Thanks be to God that prayer and counseling helped me to get my life on track.

Dina

DINA UNFILTERED
HURT PEOPLE HURT PEOPLE

Dina, one of the most resonant moments in this piece is when you speak to your grandmother and she silences you. Can you bring us into that moment?

My grandmother believed that children should be seen and not heard. She believed that children would lie and make up things on adults they didn't like, so unfortunately, before I could get the story out of my mouth good, I was being shushed and told to "stop that lying and go somewhere and play." So, I was not ever heard by my grandmother, and because of that very moment, I saw him as a man with power. I believed what he told me, that no one would believe me, and it seemed he was right. I had the feeling, *What do I do now?*

Later in life, did you report the crime?
As it relates to my uncle, the deacon, no, I didn't. I was so afraid that I would not be believed. I had already tried to tell my grandmother, and she thought I was making it up. So surely no one else was going to believe me.

As it relates to men who broke into my apartment later: Yes, I did report it to the police, but it was a total waste of time. The police made me feel as if I caused it, somehow. By asking me what I was wearing, had I been drinking, what I did—now mind you, they broke into my apartment while I was in there, asleep. I was humiliated by those who were there to protect and serve.

Did you ever wonder why the police reacted the way they did?
You know what? I've been wondering why. The irony of it: When I first was picked up to go to the police station, before going to the hospital, we were going downtown, and it was a man and a woman cop. And neither one was very sensitive. Or very compassionate. I found it to be very strange. Not so much at the time. I mean, I wasn't thinking about it then, but later, you wonder why—male or female—would they not find some sense of compassion? It was more about just going through the motions. Filling out the report.

If you could make one universal policy regarding how sexual assaults are handled, what would it be?
Immediately put the victims with someone who will validate the tragedy. Then help them process what they are going through immediately after the incident.

There's a point in the story where you ponder what made the deacon, your uncle, an abusive manipulative man. Did you ever get any insight into that?
No, I never did, but often what I thought is this: I've often thought that the church happens to be a place of trust, and they let children run free because you have this sense of it being okay. And because

he was a manipulative man, he used that to his advantage. As simple as that. They lull you into a silence because of who they represent. I didn't find out until years later that I was not his only victim. The irony of it all is that none of us ever talk about it.

So you know the other victims? Were they family members, too?
They were family members. And in our family, if something is told in confidence, it's kept in confidence. That's the problem with this whole subject. We've all kept the silence. The silence has been the death of us, and it has been the thing that allowed him to continue. We can't allow "him" to continue.

At one point, you talk about self-destructive behavior and that you tried to manipulate guys—and came close to getting yourself killed on more than one occasion. Would you be able to elaborate on that?
It's just—I'd like to not go into it. However, it does simply mean: You find yourself in a situation where you don't really trust most people. And so, you don't even understand how you are dealing with it. You find yourself in situations where you are manipulating men the way you want—because it's about control. And then, as you find yourself trying to manipulate situations, you don't really know how to handle yourself and find yourself in a world of hurt.

How did you break the cycle?
I did not recognize that I was in a cycle. In my first marriage, something would happen, and my husband would say, "You trippin'." It made me question why I was feeling the way I was. He said, "You need to go and get some help." And I went and sought out a therapist. At the time, I said, "We'll go through therapy together." But he said he wouldn't go. I was really offended by that, but I went. It started a journey of seeing I had some real issues with this stuff. Other people can see it, but you can't. It becomes a lifestyle for you.

So it sounds like you had a good experience with therapy?
I think I had a pretty good therapist. I'm a talker and I think that helps me a lot. I don't sit back and dwell on what has happened. I can get stuck there for a little while, but my normal behavior makes it so I won't get stuck there long. Just keep moving and trust in the fact that it's going to work itself out . . . and it does.

If you could give a piece of advice to a teen or kid in the same situation, what would it be?
What happened to you was wrong and painful on every level, and there is no excuse. It should have never happened to you, but it did. Unfortunately, hurt people hurt people. The person who hurt you was a person who did not know how to handle their own hurt and took it out on you. That's not an excuse to hurt you, but a reason why they did. But don't you let their poor behavior, that caused you pain, define your life. You define your life. You rise above them, and you reach out and get help. Get someone to help you process this and teach you how to grow beyond this, and don't allow this experience to cause you to be a hurt person who will eventually hurt someone else.

DINA TODAY

Dina Black did nine years in the US Air Force as a contract worker. After that she ran the family business at the Hancock Wholesale Candy and Tobacco Company, one of the first licensed black tobacco companies in Ohio, which was started by her grandfather. After that, Dina has been doing a little bit of everything, including insurance, real estate, and transporting cars. She is a busy grandma of two.

WOMAN-UP
By IMANI CAPRI

A great revolution in just one single individual will help achieve a change in the destiny of a society and, further, will enable a change in the destiny of humankind.
—Daisaku Ikeda

I was about ten years old the first time I experienced physical violation. I awakened to my mother's boyfriend squeezing my breast after he, my mother, and I had all fallen asleep while watching a movie. I was stunned. I didn't know what to do. I couldn't scream. I was just paralyzed.

He wasn't a stranger. He certainly didn't present himself as a monster. He was a graduate of an Ivy League college, an officer in the US Army Reserves, had a black belt in martial arts, and was a sexual predator.

This was a man whom I had grown to love, who became a father figure to me, and whom my mother seemed to love very much. This man violated my young, barely budding breast along with my hard-won trust. I knew what he did was wrong, but I wrestled with how to tell my mom because I knew it would ruin her happiness. The sudden weight that I felt on my shoulders as a child was incredible.

I waited a day or two and then finally told her. We were sitting in my mother's small, yellow hatchback car. I took three deep breaths, a big gulp, and every ounce of courage I could muster.

"Mom, I have to tell you something," I said. "The other night, when me, you, and your boyfriend were all watching TV and fell asleep, he squeezed my breast under my shirt, and it woke me up. I was so shocked. I didn't know what to do."

My mother was silent for a few moments. Her face was a combination of shock and disappointment. She hugged me and said, "Okay. I will talk to him."

I remember standing in the kitchen of my maternal grandmother's home. My mother, her boyfriend, and I were all there.

As my mother began relaying what I told her, nothing could have prepared me or my young heart for what happened next.

He walked over to the telephone and picked it up. "I made a mistake, but here you go. Call. If you feel that what I did was so wrong, just pick up this phone. You can call the cops. The phone is right here. I messed up, but it won't happen again," he said.

There he was taunting both my mother and I while admitting that he had grabbed my breast. That was, perhaps, the beginning of a vicious cycle of emotional and mental manipulation that would last and hang as a fog over our lives for a very long time to follow.

I was certain she was going to leave him. I was wrong. That's when I knew that I had no choice. My only choice, so I thought, was to survive. Not only did "it" happen again, but his violation of me worsened and continued. He used to tell me that if I told, people wouldn't understand, that they would look at me like I was a dirty girl. I didn't know what to believe. I was so confused. I felt dirty. I knew what he was doing was not right, but I felt like I just had to deal with it. At least I had some kind of dad, I thought, since my biological father wasn't very consistent in my life.

By the time I was eleven, he had already begun raping me. By the time I was twelve, he and my mother were married. By the time I was thirteen, my mother, then pregnant, caught him getting ready to rape me. But still, nothing happened to change our circumstance.

My teen years were a mix of emotions and experiences. Despite the reality of what had been happening to me at home, I continued to excel in school, so much so that I received a full scholarship to the same elite college-prep high school that my stepfather had attended: St. George's School in Newport, Rhode Island. I enrolled in St. George's School at fifteen years old, as a freshman, and embarked upon a new journey.

Academically, I was being challenged and prepared to start college in an Ivy League environment. My classmates were students from all over the United States and from countries across the world. They were the children of politicians, very successful businesspeople, old-money families, philanthropists, and celebrities.

On a personal level, going away to St. George's was an escape. It gave me a chance to have a life of my own, somewhat removed from my stepfather's immediate grasp, and since St. George's is a college-prep school, I lived at school, in a dorm, and only went home on vacations for holidays.

Each day, I would go to class, have some sort of sports or theater activity after classes ended, and then do homework and hang out with friends in the evening. High school at St. George's did have its challenges, too, like being one of six African American females out of a student body of almost four hundred. There were cultural challenges and definitely economic challenges. I wasn't poor, but I certainly didn't come from legacy millionaires like most of my counterparts. But I did well in school. I was elected to student council several years in a row and also became president of the Poetry Club.

I never told anyone about the abuse I had experienced or that it continued when I went home on vacation. I lived a double life.

But one experience at school captured this paradox perfectly.

As president of the Poetry Club, and a member of the school's Multicultural Committee, I had the privilege and opportunity to help choose the keynote speaker for the school's centennial celebration. We chose Dr. Maya Angelou. Although I was among a group of people selected to meet and speak with Dr. Angelou before her speech the night of our centennial celebration, that meeting was canceled due to her driver getting lost on their way to our event.

I was very disappointed, but I made my way to the auditorium where she was scheduled to speak. My stepfather, who came up to the school to attend the celebration, was also with me.

For some reason, I began pacing the hall as people were seated in the auditorium. At one point, a side door opened. Maya Angelou walked straight down the very hall that I had been pacing, and directly toward me, as though we had an appointment. She stood in front of me, statuesque, with a warm and broad smile. She extended her hands to me and held my hands in hers for a few moments. My heart was pounding as she looked into my eyes. My stepfather scurried to my side as Dr. Angelou said to me, "You are so beautiful."

She looked toward my stepfather and asked, "Is she your daughter?"

"Yes, yes," he responded.

Dr. Angelou said, "She is beautiful. You have no idea how beautiful she is."

I wanted to scream. I wanted to tell her, "He's raping me and has been since I was a little girl." But I couldn't say anything. I was paralyzed. I was overwhelmed by the entire moment.

Yet her words spoke life into my heart. Her words made me feel like she saw me, my heart, and maybe even my pain and my possibility in just those few moments. She squeezed my hands again and then made her way toward the stage.

She told her own story. She spoke of the rape she experienced as a child and how she later became mute.

I was seventeen. Later that night, my stepfather raped me.

By the time I was nineteen, I left home, lived with, and engaged in a relationship with my stepfather's relative in exchange for physical protection. Ironically, my stepfather's relative, who was twenty-plus years older than me and whom I told about my stepfather's abuse, was the only adult I ever saw who was unafraid of and not physically intimidated by my stepfather. Eventually, once I was away from all of the dysfunction, I felt incredible, indescribable rage. I realized that I had not really been properly protected at all. I had been isolated from members of my mother's and my biological father's family for years. I didn't know how to even begin to ask for help, and I was too ashamed to admit what had happened to me and how I was being protected. I felt hopeless, betrayed, damaged, and abandoned.

Instead of numbing the pain with drugs or alcohol, I coped by staying busy. If I piled my plate with jobs, school, and other activities, then I didn't have time to sulk—that was my thinking. I volunteered with the AmeriCorps program to earn money for college. Later, I was hired as a teaching assistant at a local elementary school. I also took on a part-time job as a bilingual sales representative of AT&T and even found a way to squeeze in college classes a few nights per week. I began learning how to salsa dance, and that became one of my favorite pastimes. When I danced, I could forget everything and just lose myself in the music.

It took years for me to truly confront all of that inner hurt, but eventually I did. Being introduced to Nichiren Buddhism through chanting the phrase *Nam-myoho-renge-kyo* was the catalyst.

At the age of twenty-two, I began studying Nichiren Buddhism with an organization called the Soka Gakkai International. My practice of Nichiren Buddhism literally began to shift my life. Studying Buddhism taught me that my life had value and that I had the power to change my life from the inside out. I remember reading a passage written by former Soka Gakkai president Josei Toda. He explained that when people who had experienced great tragedy in their lives began practicing Nichiren Buddhism, they would come to understand that all of their tragedies were really tools to help them to fulfill a major life purpose of encouraging others through their personal victories. I cried and cried after reading that passage. His words made sense to me. It was like a floodlight shone and the purpose of my pain was revealed to me.

It also taught me that I could even use the "sludge" in my life as nourishment for a beautiful life, just like the lotus blossom that yields glorious petals by pulling up nutrients from the muddiest swamp. In fact, it was said that the more muddy the swamp, the more beautiful the lotus flower.

Two years later, at twenty-four, I had a nervous breakdown. All of the pain, hurt, anger, and rage that I had been suppressing and ignoring by staying busy finally erupted. Although it was a nervous breakdown, it became my spiritual breakthrough. After spending a week in the hospital, I realized and resolved that it was time for me to "woman-up" and face what I was feeling head on.

A series of major life changes occurred after that: I moved back to my childhood home and lived with my maternal grandmother in Bedford, Ohio. I enrolled in Kent State University full-time and continued working to earn my bachelor's degree in broadcast journalism. While in college, I also pursued legal charges against my stepfather for the years that he raped me while we lived in Ohio. The Cleveland Rape Crisis Center helped me to confirm that, despite my being an adult, I was still within the statute of limitations to pursue justice for the violations that happened to me as a child. I also began rigorous therapy. None of this was easy, but I made the decision to take my life back, to take total responsibility for my healing and transformation.

I was a full-time student, working several jobs, when a Cleveland grand jury decided to indict my stepfather. Although he and my mother, and two siblings, were living in a different state then, the trial would be in Ohio. Despite the fear and intimidation of my past,

I had finally found the courage to stand up for the wounded little girl whom I had been carrying with me for more than a decade.

After two trials, the first of which was dismissed due to a hung jury, twelve jurors convicted my stepfather for repeatedly raping me as a child. He was sentenced to a minimum of twenty to twenty-five years in prison before being eligible for parole, with a requirement to register as a sex offender for the remainder of his life upon his release.

A year later, almost to the exact date of my stepfather's sentencing, I graduated college with a bachelor's degree in broadcast journalism. I immediately enrolled in graduate school and received my master's degree in digital storytelling and marketing in December 2011.

During my undergraduate and graduate years, I also started using my voice, telling my story. I spoke in numerous venues, appeared in local, national, and international media outlets, participated in training seminars for law-enforcement officials, and sought ways to use my voice to help empower others. Also during that time, my mother and two younger siblings, with whom I had not had a relationship for at least ten years, came back into my life. My mother apologized to me for not protecting me as a child and explained that she, too, had been raped as a child but never told anyone. I realized that my actions broke a cycle. She thanked me for my courage because my standing up and fighting helped to free her, too. As we began the work of healing together and creating a new relationship, she also joined me in telling my story, our story. My mother also divorced my abuser.

Today, I have an amazing life. Both of my biological parents are active participants in it. I have wonderful, growing relationships with all of my siblings. I am dating a man who supports the work I am doing to help bring change in the world. I am currently building two separate ventures, the Courage 2 Change Total Life Empowerment and the Capri Project, which will both be dedicated to helping girls and women to identify and create an empowered relationship with their own inner greatness. I continue to practice Nichiren Buddhism and seek ways that I can continue using my voice.

More important to me, though, is what I have learned and continue to learn: Whether you have been raped or not, we all experience disappointments, some sort of pain to one degree or another. But we have a choice: We can allow ourselves to become "defined" by what happens to us, or we can choose to take whatever we have experienced in our lives and turn it into something to fuel our own healing, our personal growth and transformation. My story changed because I changed. I broke the silence and literally set my life free, and when I did that, I brought my family with me. When I chose to speak, I saved myself and those around me. I will never underestimate my strength or inner power again.

IMANI UNFILTERED
UNSTOPPABLE GRACE

Imani, this is a truly inspirational story. Your positive attitude and practice seem to provide a good balance for your life. How are things now?
Recovering from sexual abuse has taken years, almost two decades. Most people, including survivors, sometimes don't realize the layers of healing that may be necessary after experiencing sexually related trauma, especially over an extended period of time. Recovery is an evolving journey. A person may think he or she is fully healed, and then something can trigger a traumatic memory and he or she has to choose how to handle it. The real healing and recovery comes in being able to not give those memories or triggers any negative, destructive power over how you view yourself or how you decide to live your life. I do feel recovered.

You mention living a double life while you were at St. George's. Do you know if any of your friends ever suspected anything at all?
To my knowledge, no. I don't think any of my friends suspected anything. If they did, they never approached me. I'm still in contact with many of them. I remember revealing to some of them what I had experienced, and they were blown away. You know what is also interesting: Within the last year or two, the *Boston Globe* broke some

stories about sexual abuse in college prep schools, and St. George's, ironically enough, was one of the main schools involved.

You talk a little bit about your journey helping yourself and helping your mom. What was it like to foster that relationship? Was there a lot of baggage to unpack?
Basically, yeah. There was a period of time when I first left home, I was engaged in this weird relationship with one of my ex-stepfather's relatives, and we were all living in the same city. So I would run into my mom in public, and we wouldn't speak, and I had two younger siblings. It was really awkward. We didn't speak for maybe ten years. Then I ended up having a nervous breakdown while she was deployed in Iraq. My health insurance got a hold of her. She called. We weren't talking about the issues, but we were talking. It took time.

In 2011, my maternal grandmother, my rock my entire life, was diagnosed with breast cancer. My mom hadn't been talking to anybody. Then out of the blue she just happened to reach out to my grandmother without knowing she had a diagnosis. Christmas 2011, my grandmother told her, "You need to call Imani."

In 2012, she and I ended up talking. Around Valentine's day, we had our first conversation. By that time, we had gone through the two trials, but I had done all this work on myself, and during that ten or so years, I'd grown. Whatever it was that my mom had gone through, we were able to meet in a space where the bitterness was gone. I didn't have the bitterness in my heart, and she was in a place where she was apologetic. What's interesting, when we started speaking, my mom was really looking for something to make her more whole and complete. I just started talking to her about Nichiren Buddhism. Lo and behold, she was interested. She got connected with a local group, and we talked more frequently. She came and visited me with my sister, who I'd last seen when she was, maybe, one. They came to Ohio, as a surprise, to visit my grandmother. It was a heartfelt family reunion. They eventually moved back to Ohio. At one point we were all living in my grandmother's house, which was difficult. We had to navigate this shit on so many levels. So many layers.

Still, the universe brought us to a space where we had a common ground. Eventually, I asked her: "Why didn't you protect me?"

She broke down and confided in me that she had been molested when she was young. She said, "I didn't protect you because I didn't know how to protect myself."

Just hearing my mom say that—and seeing her sobbing—I realized that she did the best she knew how based on her own life experience.

Now when people see my mom and I, we have a much better relationship. It's very organic. She's supportive of how I use my voice. And when I chose to share my story for a wider cause, she participated and shared her perspective.

Speaking of using your story in a larger sense, you mentioned that you did training with law enforcement. What was that like? Were they receptive?

I did one summit for police chiefs in Cuyahoga County, Ohio, where I was invited to share my story. Later, I participated in a training for two hundred Cuyahoga County prosecutors.

Consistently, they were deeply moved, deeply touched and impacted. The first time, when I spoke in front of the police chiefs, I had never had an audience that was predominantly older white men. I was unsure of how they would receive my story and my message. I'm an African American woman. I was really surprised by how some people in the audience were really moved.

When I participated in the continuing legal education training, a good percentage of the prosecutors were also white male, but the audience, as a whole, was more diverse. People responded. I could see their hearts were touched. We talked about the process, the two trials. I was trying to encourage the prosecutors to usher someone through a transformative experience—to acknowledge that the prosecutor is a guardian and is helping the survivor step into another level of personal empowerment. Any survivor who chooses to pursue charges or tell his or her story or use his or her voice in service of others is taking a huge, powerful, healing, courageous, and selfless step. If the prosecutors support that, they might get different results. I don't think a lot of them were typically approaching their cases in that fashion. I continuously encouraged them to acknowledge a deeper level of humanity and compassion, which would allow victims to open up and overcome personal fears. By doing this, they might share more details and help law enforcement make stronger cases.

Last question, you were president of the Poetry Club. Do you want to share any of your poetry with us?
I wrote this while I was in high school in 1996:

"Dance"
There I was swayin' to the beat
as my spirit played out its song by way of my feet.
Completely entranced, in my own little dance,
turnin', slidin', shakin', glidin', oh here we go again.
Seems like my spirit began to fly, yeah she was soarin' high.
So I stood back & let her do her thing,
lookin' at how that body would swing,
almost like I could see her partner,
but her stare went far beyond her.
What a wonderful way to dance across the place,
Oh yeah baby, my spirit had grace.

IMANI TODAY

Imani Capri is an experienced speaker and award-winning writer who is on a mission to change the culture of silence, shame, and judgment that shrouds the issue of sexual abuse. She has appeared in local Cleveland news media, such as WKYC, WEWS, the Ohio News Network, Kentwired.com, and WERE FM. She has been featured in a violence-prevention training video course for Green Dot. She has been published in the *Christian Science Monitor,* the *Canton Repository Newspaper,* the nationally distributed Buddhist publications *Living Buddhism* magazine and the *World Tribune Newspaper,* and on the website of the Chicago-based Voices and Faces Project. Imani has been a featured speaker for the Cleveland Rape Crisis Center's Youth 360 program, the Cuyahoga County Executive Summit with Police Chiefs, Specialized Alternatives for Families and Youth (Cleveland), the Laurel School, the Cuyahoga

County Prosecutor's Office, and Soka Gakkai International USA.

Imani holds a bachelor's degree in broadcast journalism and a master of liberal studies degree in digital storytelling and marketing from Kent State University. In her nine-to-five life, Imani works in a litigation department of a law firm. You can find her online at www.imanicapri.com.

SATURDAYS

By JENNIFER CARMER-HALL

It was warm that Saturday morning in late August when my
parents dropped me downtown on their way to the first Iowa
State football game of the season. I told them I needed to go in
to work for an hour or two and would hang out with friends until
they returned to pick me up that afternoon. That was a lie. I actually
planned to go to the church to meet the new minister and see if he
could help me. My friend Margy said he was nice and I would like
him. I hoped she was right because I didn't see any other options.
I wasn't supposed to be this miserable. My parents were successful
and well-liked. I was a gifted athlete and a top student. And yet, I felt
ugly and rejected. I was no one's best friend, not even close. I was
that extra person at the party, the one you played pranks on, never
the one you confided your secrets with. And then there was my arm.
I was born one-handed, missing the right arm just below the elbow.
And despite the best cosmetic, bionic prostheses money could buy, I
was considered damaged goods by boys in my school. Nobody's best
friend; certainly not anyone's girlfriend.

When they dropped me off, I pretended to go up to the radio
station where I worked. I waited in the hallway until I was sure they
were out of sight, and then I headed to the church a few blocks away.
There was a hot August breeze picking up, and I could hear it roaring
in and through the massive maple trees on the church lawn. The air
felt heavy with humidity and smelled of Iowa farm dirt. I felt even
heavier, dragging all my problems with me. *I shouldn't be here, airing
my dirty laundry, but something has to give and someone has to help.*
Someone had to know what it was really like to be me. *What if someone
sees me? What if they ask me what I am doing at the church on a Saturday
morning?* I couldn't just say it was because I was thinking of hurting
myself. I couldn't trust anyone but a minister with that.

The wood-framed glass door to the church office was tucked
beneath an alcove, behind a concrete porch. The church offices
had lived a previous life as the historical parsonage, which hugged

the back wall of the sanctuary. The hybrid building was designed originally to house the minister and his family and had "secret passages" and back stairways to allow him to travel to and from work without going outside. When I turned the handle and pushed the heavy, old door over the hardwood floor, the glass panel shuddered and rattled, echoing in the empty foyer. I was sure I had disturbed this holy place. I considered turning around and running away before I was noticed, but instead I entered. His office was just around the corner, and as I tiptoed to it, still unsure of my plan, I noticed the door was slightly open and the light was on. I knocked timidly on the walnut door and heard him say, "Come in." His office was a mess: boxes of books everywhere and mostly empty bookshelves waiting to be filled. He was standing with chin in hand behind his massive desk, which was also temporarily accommodating unshelved books and folders, contemplating, what seemed to be, something important. His eyes twinkled at the sight of me and a big grin crossed his face. "To what do I owe this pleasure!?" "Hi," I eeked out. "I'm Jennifer. I was just in the area and wanted to come say hi. My friend Margy said she met you, and you were nice, and would be easy to talk to."

"Well, have a seat, Jennifer," he gestured toward a chair, the only uncovered space in the room. "What would you like to talk about?"

I offered to come back another time. I could see how busy he was. He insisted that I stay, and so I did. And as I started to tell him all the reasons I had come, the tears started to flow. Out they came ... like water gushing from a broken hydrant. I wept. He listened. I wept some more. I described my fears, anxieties, and woes for over an hour. At the end of my visit, he hugged me long and hard and told me that he hoped I would come back. He said he was glad that I came on a Saturday morning. Saturdays were a good time to visit, he added, because it was quiet in the church, and he could spend more time with me.

When I returned the following Saturday, I was already feeling he was doing me a huge favor—an important man spending time to help me. I barely knew him, yet he seemed to know me better than anyone ever had. I couldn't get enough of him. I kept going back. Monday through Friday became solely a means to get to Saturdays. He assigned me "projects" so I could tell my parents I was volunteering at the church, and no one would wonder why I was spending so much time there.

He began touching me on the hips, buttocks, and small of my

back shortly after he met me. And yet it never occurred to me he was doing this intentionally to test me . . . to screen me. Each time it seemed like an awkward accident, maybe even a misperception on my part. Maybe they did things differently where he came from. *Did he really just do that?* I often asked myself. It's not like he started with sexual touching or groping. He started by steadying me as I stumbled or lost my balance. When we walked through a doorway together, we constantly bumped into each other. It could have been an accident. No one had ever talked to me about rape. People had talked to me about respecting my elders, and the importance of not crossing an adult in charge, but no one had talked to me about how abusers groom victims. It was easy, at first, to discount everything that seemed awkward.

He was so very patient. Making me feel important by asking me to be his personal tour guide for his new church, asking for my opinion about decisions he had to make, and subtly caressing me when he talked to me in private. He made me feel more special and powerful than anyone ever had. One day, while I was in his office, alone with him, he told me the church board was considering converting some of the empty upstairs offices into additional Sunday school space, and he wondered what I thought about it. No adult had ever asked my opinion on something like that. I replied that I thought it could work well.

"Let's go check it out," he said.

We walked upstairs with me leading, and him with his hand gently on my back. Something I had grown accustomed to. We stood in the middle of the room, near enough to touch, but not touching, turning slowly around surveying the room that used to be a bedroom in the top floor of the parsonage. We imagined couches and comfy chairs would make the junior high kids feel good about meeting there. As we turned, I could smell his English Leather cologne wafting through his crisp, clean shirt, and I began to sense that we were lingering there. He told me how much he appreciated my help and how special I was, and then he offered me a hug, which I accepted. I slipped into his arms and felt I had finally found someone who really, truly appreciated and loved me just as I was. As we embraced, I breathed in his musky cologne. Then slowly, gently, he took hold of the hand I had wrapped around his waist and gave it a gentle nudge.

He guided my hand downward and around his hip, then down further in between us. My hand came to rest awkwardly on his inner thigh, and then he went back to hugging me. I was mortified. What was happening? My mind raced with possibilities—none of them involved him doing something wrong. *Maybe his back hurts and he wanted to move my hand, but he accidentally put it in this weird place. Maybe I moved my hand farther than he meant me to, and he was too nice to say something.* He was probably as embarrassed as I was, I thought.

I thought wrong.

What I would learn, later, is that this is how a master predator grooms a victim. This is what no one talks about.

By the time his touches became more obvious, it occurred to me that I had been allowing it (or something similar) for weeks. To reject his touches at that point seemed hypocritical, and I was still unsure of my perceptions. So I began working on an alternate storyline to make sense of what was happening. I told myself he must be trying to tell me something with his guided touching. I remembered my mother telling me as a young girl that "someday I would meet a special man who loved me, and he would touch me in a special way."

Once I became invested in a story where he was simply in love with me and unable to express it, I actually began helping him abuse me. I kissed him in the hallway to see if he would kiss back. When he did, I told him I loved him, and he told me he loved me back. The stage was set, the door was open. And then, only then, did the full sexual contact begin. By the time we had intercourse—six months after that first Saturday—I actually thought that, at fifteen years old, I had seduced a thirty-eight-year-old man. All of this made sense because everyone had talked about falling in love, but no one had talked to me about rape. It may have been easier to pretend he loved me and that I seduced him, but it trapped me inside a story that didn't add up.

It would be decades later before I could see it for what it really was—rape.

Several years later, when I started to speak out about what happened to me, I met a woman who was abused by the same pastor. I'd already realized the truth, but when I met her, it clarified it for me: What I had experienced wasn't love or respect. It wasn't even special. I was a child, looking for guidance. He was a predator, looking for his next victim.

JENNIFER UNFILTERED
UNPACKING TRUTH

Jennifer, this story has many layers of manipulation. What would you like to say to a teen or kid in your situation, who might be having a similar thought process?

Wanting to be loved and cherished is not wrong. It's a basic human need, not a luxury. You don't owe an adult anything in return for loving you or paying attention to you. Love is not a transaction you pay for or earn by doing something in return. Don't let any adult make you believe it is.

Let's talk about recovery. Once you realized what had happened, were you able to move past it?

Recovery was and is a long, slow process. I started recovering the first time I told someone what happened to me. But even though I was healing and getting better, I continued to choose unhealthy partners and even get revictimized many times over the next thirty years. I do feel that, today, I am in a very healthy state. I have worked hard to get here. Recovery isn't what I thought it would be, though. I wanted recovery to mean that I could be totally free from the past, but I still get triggered often. The difference now is that the triggers inform me and protect me. I have learned to listen to my inner voice and accept that I know things I can't unknow.

Did you run into any barriers?

The biggest barrier to my recovery was thinking that what happened to me was special, unique, "a relationship." The first time I told someone, I didn't report a crime, I confessed a sin. I said I was having an affair with the minister. Unfortunately, the person I told was another minister. Actually, I told several other ministers, and they all reacted the same. They took my confession and helped me work on my guilt. It wasn't until I told a female therapist that I made significant progress in healing because she told me the truth—that it wasn't my fault and that I had been raped.

Was there a breakthrough moment where you knew you would be okay?
I had a dream several years ago. I dreamed I was standing in a crowded hotel lobby with people milling about and crossing through the crowd. Suddenly, I spotted my abuser standing in a doorway on the opposite side of the lobby. I pushed my way through the crowd. I was on my way to attack him, but feeling all sorts of conflicting emotions—hate, fear, attraction, rage, compassion. When I reached him, we were magically transported to a peaceful garden, where he introduced me to a young woman and then he walked off. I sat down and talked to the woman. She was kind, funny, intelligent, and wise. When I woke up, I realized that the woman was me, and that despite everything he had done to me, I was going to be okay. In fact, better than okay.

Are you there? Is everything okay now?
Yes. I live a very, very rich life. And because I started speaking about my truth, I am free to live an authentic life.

JENNIFER TODAY

Jennifer Carmer-Hall worked in the financial planning field for over twenty-five years. She also volunteers as a CASA (Court-Appointed Special Advocates for Children) caseworker in Nebraska, where she lives with her husband and children. Jennifer cofounded LearningHope.org with Jackie Gutschenritter. LearningHope.org is a web-based resource for survivors of childhood sexual abuse. She is a regular contributor to the site's blog, as well as a motivational speaker.

I WANT TO STAY ALIVE
By JOAN CLARE

It was all clear that Saturday, no snow on the ground. Trace and I moved from our homes in the Chicago suburbs to a brick building on Kenmore, at the corner of Waveland, across from the Wrigley Field ballpark. I thought it would improve my lot. I was too old to be a runaway at eighteen, but I ran so fast to Kenmore, that wanderlust feeling was there. I was in between—in between high school and college. On the move to life.

Everything in Chicago was made of brick—an outcome of the Great Fire of 1871 when Chicago forced a bill that all buildings must be made in brick. It was cool—and the reason I loved the city—because the architecture was everywhere. It made me feel that I was drifting back into the nineteenth century. Once I saw a little girl dressed up in Sunday clothes from a century before, with a parasol, carrying a doll, trying to cross the street. I looked one more time, and she was gone. I never saw her again. I read years later she "lived" in Graceland Cemetery, a little farther over and beyond from our apartment. She was a ghost who needed to go out and play.

In Chicago, the ghosts came and found you.

As I wandered the streets, I would dream back to being a different person, thinking that maybe shaking off the suburbs would create a new me. As the days of living went by, Trace found out I was the worst kind of roommate. The one who didn't pay her share of the rent, $175, on time, brought stray men home, smoked weed continuously, scribbled in a notebook, and declared I was an artist now.

I'd listen to Blondie and all the songs on *Parallel Lines* in my new living room. But one song, "11:59" was the undercurrent in my head: "Take it down the freeway like a bullet to the ocean. . . . Today can last another million years / Today could be the end of me / It's 11:59, and I want to stay alive."

My past imperfect was a breakup with my boyfriend in my hometown right before I moved, and I felt abandoned. I had big plans, but I also thought he would get married to me. How did I know I suffered from borderline personality disorder? I was inclined to fainting spells, crying spells, emotional storms, depression, and then pretending like it never happened. I became a person my friends did not know.

But I was way over my friends.

I had to be; the contempt they had for me was incredible. I was tall, blue eyed, very skinny, like junky skinny, and already into the heroin chic mode. But I found Broadway Street, closer to the Lake, saw the gay people, the transgender people, the homeless people, and I was home.

You could be a drug addict, a homeless person, a drug dealer, a greasy whore, or a guy who flips pancakes. If you didn't get a college degree, there was simply nothing in between. I felt I was already marginalized as a female and a teenager, by friends, family, and myself, so it was a little hard to find a direction. I also knew I was on the brink of a nervous breakdown, and I left home in time to hide it.

What I was doing, skipping here, skipping there, in and out of college, was because of emotional problems, suicidal tendencies, drug abuse. Was I fit for college? The administrators said no, but I ignored them and went on to get a higher education.

One of the classes I took was Intro to Shakespeare. I was swimming along in class when we started reading *Henry IV, Part 2*. I made the mistake of asking if it was set in the Hundred Years War (1337–1453) or the War of the Roses (1455–1485). The male professor let me know with just a look on his face that he was embarrassed that anyone would be stupid enough to ask a question like that. He smacked the wee paperback of *Henry IV*. The entire class was silent. The professor was implying we were a dumb bunch of bums, but a quick look at the dates shows he was probably hiding his own lack of historical knowledge. Such was the college experience.

One school day, I had my fuchsia blouse on, a favorite because of the gathering in the center front. The V neck, and the cap sleeves, made me look street but slightly glam. I thought I looked normal. It never occurred to me that being underweight, with a glazed look in my eyes, and bad posture, really, genuinely made me look like a junkie in the city lights.

Just as I was going through the turnstile to get on the elevated train to yet another lecture, a guy around my age pegged me.

"Hay," he said.

"Yeah?" I said, after dropping my quarters in the pay slot.

"Want some weed?"

I did. "Yeah, sure."

"Okay, follow me."

We walked out of the Addison el station about a half block down Sheridan Street and came to this transient hotel— a ratty, rundown place—most especially the light teal carpet that looked fifty years old, and I started to have my doubts. But my need clouded my sense. Copping dope was always a ringy situation and part of the allure.

"Come on," he said, smooth as silk, "it's really good stuff, man, nothing to be afraid of, man."

So I went with him in my haze and walked into the room.

After I was in, he slammed the door. He pointed to a little couch and told me to go sit down. I did, but my hypervigilance—which started when I was twelve, when I was sexually molested by three guys in a tree fort—made me freeze on the couch, and I sussed the situation out. There was probably no way of creeping around him without getting killed.

He came over and made a fist in my face, and some spirit surged in me, my hidden anger blasting out. I got up. I looked him in the eye. "Don't you fucking touch me, you son of a bitch," I said.

How bad can this be if I'm saving my own life, I thought. (Answer: very bad.)

Problem was, maybe I was looking for an end to my useless life, or thought I deserved it. When all your friends tell you what a loser you are, no matter what you do, the desire to die is a realistic choice.

I pulled off the fuchsia blouse, and all my clothes, and made a point of getting on the bed. The confusion of living or dying was so tight, it trapped the anger and fear in me. He shrugged his shoulders and took my cue. I later found out he was a just-released felon from Cook County Jail.

It would have been a good move to throw up in his face. Instead, I looked out the window and around for an angel, but none were to be found, so my mind came back. Then he grunted, and got off of me, put on his clothes, and went for my purse. Got the only money I had, a twenty. Then he split.

I put on my clothes, grabbed my purse, walked out the door, and scurried down the grubby flight of stairs. When I hit daylight everything was a blur. I realized I had left my glasses upstairs. I had no idea where they were. As I steeled myself to walk back to the scene of the crime, the angel I was looking for appeared from a basement apartment. It was a regular handyman guy.

"Was there some kind of trouble, miss?"

I told him yes. But right away I decided not to mention being raped. I mean, was I?

"I'll call the police," he said.

He did, and they came. I reported a strong-arm robbery. Even the two cops knew I was lying, given the way I looked. Scared, I guess. I could tell they were relieved I didn't make it a rape case, but they made up for it by being nice and telling me to buy my hooch at the Lake Front in the future.

They drove me back to my apartment, said they'd be in touch.

I went to my bed and cuddled with my two cats. Not long after that I went back out to the Addison el liqueur store and bought a ninety-eight-cent bottle of beer. I was too young, but this guy always sold it to me. You know, in Chicago, no one denies you a beer.

When I came home, I drank it down in two swallows. I wondered if anyone would really care given that I messed around with strangers all the time since I moved to the city. That brick girdle I planted around my hips shoved away a lot of the "what ifs."

So, I just put on another Blondie album: *Eat to the Beat.*

"'Cause I'm not here, and you're not there / and I'm not living in the real world / I'm not living in the real world . . . / Didn't I ever tell you I was gone?"

JOAN UNFILTERED
LOVE, SISTER, IT'S JUST A KISS AWAY

This is a complex story, Joan. So many things go wrong very quickly. How did you come to the realization that it was rape?
In 1980, rape was only considered a crime if there was a deadly weapon involved. No one would believe you if you let the guy rape you and there was no physical violence. I kept it to myself, but I knew it was rape right away, even if I questioned it later, because it made me sick to my stomach, and it was a horrible experience.

You mention borderline personality disorder, or BPD. Were you ever diagnosed or treated for a mental illness?
In May 2016, when I first submitted this story to you, I was being treated for BPD. BPD is a condition that springs from life upsets, family traits, lack of empathy, and chronic health problems. This is my personal observation after daily attendance in group therapy for five weeks.

You did mention, in passing, that there was a situation in the treehouse when you were younger. Do you think that the mental health issues, the BPD, are a result of these experiences?
I definitely think they are, plus family factors and inheritance. Absolutely. I think trauma was a big part of it. There's a great book, to that end. It's called *Trauma and Recovery: The Aftermath of Violence—From Domestic Abuse to Political Terror* by Judith L. Herman.

What else has worked well in recovery?
Group therapy. In group, BPD is most often called by an even broader name, a mood disorder. This is episodes of depression mixed with anxiety, which can change from day to day. Medication and group therapy are the best known ways to treat it. Let me add, people new to group often reject it at first. You are there for your own problems plus everyone else's. Embracing sobriety is also routinely expected. This is a tall order. It works because it strives to make you a better person.

I followed up group by creative writing about my years in high school; I tracked a lot things beginning all the way back then. This approach has worked wonders, and I am in better shape at fifty-six than ever before.

You mention that after the incident, you weren't sure if anyone would really care. Were you right about that?
Yes, silence was my way to go. As I mentioned, I just shook it off. One of my "friends" would always say to me, in that off-hand, malicious way, "Oh, you were asking for it. You walked right into it. You weren't a virgin. What difference did it make to you?"

How did this impact you?
At first, I didn't listen, but as she reminded me of the past all the time, unbelievable anger blew up in me, and I couldn't explain it. I did not understand why this person was being hateful toward me, victim blaming, and twisting facts she was unaware of—like the lineup ID at Cook County Jail, the arraignment in court, and the police coming to my apartment with a picture book to see if I could pick out the guy from fifty other mugshots. It's hard to believe there are people in your life just waiting for the opportunity to make you suffer more.

Was there a breakthrough moment in your recovery?
I had just turned nineteen years old and had that unique ability to block the crime out. Teenagers are masters at this kind of thing, but "the body always remembers." Depression, unexplained pain in my shoulder and back, migraine headaches, and my mood swings became closer and closer to each other; I started rapid cycling from hypomania to depression within hours of each other. I tried to live a normal life, and I understood I'd have to live this way. Finally, one year ago, age fifty-four, my therapist sent me to Rape Victim Advocates for counseling. When my experience was validated, that's when the breakthrough in my recovery began.

How is everything now?
When someone finally validated my experience of rape, not stupidity, at Rape Victim Advocates, I slowly let go and processed

the emotions trapped inside. One year later, I'm feeling much better, but it still haunts me that this "friend" used the crime to belittle and abuse, verbally, to break me down even further.

You quote Blondie in your story. Are there other artists or musicians who got you through hard times?
The Rolling Stones, "Gimme Shelter": "Oh a storm is threatening / My very life today / If I don't get some shelter / I'm gonna fade away . . . / Rape, murder! / It's just a shot away . . . / I tell you love, sister, it's just a kiss away."

JOAN TODAY

Joan Clare is a graduate of Columbia College Chicago's creative writing program. She devotes most of her time and energy to mental health issues and is working on a novel, *Backdoor Man,* that weaves together sexual abuse, mental health, and living in the aftermath.

RECLAMATION

By JANE COCHRANE

And this is how it starts.

We're halfway into this cheap bottle of wine, both of us have seen *Harry Potter and the Sorcerer's Stone* at least three dozen times, and don't think I haven't noticed your hand on my thigh. I can read you like Shakespeare, which is to say better than most and improving with practice, and I know damn well that I'm two kisses to your neck away from the hitch of your breath—and this is how it starts.

Someone once told me that if you're going to write a poem about sex, people should have to wonder if it's about sex. Maybe if I were classier, or a better writer, I could write that poem. But this is not that poem. This is the moment that comes about twenty-seven minutes, four position changes, and two not quite simultaneous orgasms later (but we were so close this time), and it starts with you making a lighthearted comment about the mess.

Joke all you want, but there's no business quite as messy as a girl raped at six and left alone in the back of a car to pull on panties with trembling fingers, so excuse me if the only thing I see in the "mess" of your semen is haven, because the fact that I am not trying to scrub this out from under fingernails like dried blood is proof enough that you have taught me men do not have pain etched into palms like privilege and that to touch is not always to hurt.

Anyone who claims that healing is a journey is kidding themselves. There's no one start or end point, no linear path, and sanctuary from the storms often manifests itself in places that look like a lion's den at first glance. For me, sleeping in sheets stained with your cum is the closest I've ever come to feeling like all I need is the folds of this fabric to forge something of myself again. When you're having sex with a broken girl, rule number one is you don't fuck to fix. In sunlight, when the currents and tides of the day lure us apart momentarily, it is then I am forced to admit that sex with you is not therapy. But it's a close second, and I'll be *damned* if it doesn't feel better.

And I know there are moments: moments when I flinch under fingertips that in my mind are no longer yours, and I'm sorry. But I am learning to discern certain subtleties between the exploration and colonization of my body, and you are no Columbus.

The sad truth, darling, is that I have lived with ghosts in my skin and my sock drawer longer than I have had my period, longer than I've been able to ride my bike without training wheels. There are no credits that can be expected to start rolling, no expiration date on this kind of coping. There are days when I am less stardust than sawdust, less survivor than victim, but that does not mean that the reclamation of my own body is any less eternal. And this—this slightly buzzed fuck with *Harry Potter* playing in the background, this momentary investment in a long-term endeavor, this whisper in my ear reminding me that I am so goddamn beautiful—

This is how it starts.

―――――――――

JANE UNFILTERED
REDEMPTION

Jane, to be honest, every time I read this piece, it makes me cry. One thing I find interesting is that most of the submissions to this anthology focus on what happened, but you focus on a moment much later—a moment of empowerment. Why did you choose to focus on reclamation instead of the past?

It's a pretty commonplace narrative, I think, that writing can be healing. And I completely agree with that. I just don't think writing is *inherently* healing. I think writing is hard work. I think it's demanding. I think it's exhausting. But I also think it has an immense capacity to mend and make better. You just have to want that out of your writing. So I focused on writing about a moment that felt like healing because I wanted to prove to myself that if I could inhabit that empowered mind-set long enough to write, edit, and rewrite this piece, that meant it was real. It meant I had put in the work to get better, that I viewed myself as a thing worthy of redemption. And I do. I finally, honestly, do.

I'm so glad to hear you say that. Do you mind if we talk a little bit about what happened? You write that you were six. Did you know it was rape at the time?

No. I was only six—I didn't have the vocabulary or the understanding at all. I didn't realize until I was twelve years old—we were reading Harper Lee's *To Kill a Mockingbird* in my sixth-grade English class. There's a scene where Scout asks Atticus to define rape, and his response didn't really make sense to me, so I simply looked it up in the dictionary. That wasn't just the first time I had a word for what happened to me—it's the first time I realized it was wrong. For the longest time, I always thought it was just a game the older kids played, and I had gotten mixed up in it.

In all those years up to age twelve, did you ever try to tell anyone about the situation—an adult or a friend—even though you didn't have any words for it?

No. Never. Not a word. And even after I had language to explain what happened, it was another five years before I broke my silence.

What has helped you the most in recovery, in bringing you to the days of reclamation?

I think the two things that are tied for most helpful for me are therapy and running. I am lucky enough to attend a university that provides some amazing counseling services. Even though I fought my boyfriend tooth and nail about whether or not I needed therapy in the first place, finally admitting to myself that I should at least try to get help was the most meaningful step I've taken in recovery so far. I was also lucky enough to be matched with a therapist that had a style which really helped me. (Liz, if you're reading this, please know that you saved me all over again every single Tuesday. I am forever grateful for the confidence you gave me, the confidence that I had the power to take care of myself.) For me, therapy reminded me of something I knew on a cognitive level but often forgot on a practical one: that I am deserving of love and care, and I'm not being selfish when I ask for it.

As for running, I'm by no means a marathon runner. My mile time is around eight minutes, which I'm pretty sure is about dead average. I don't do anything wild like get up at 5 a.m. and run seven miles every day. I'm not on a track team. Some mornings, I just get up, throw on my running shoes, and run around the block. But no matter how far or how fast I go, running reminds me that my body is *mine*, that it is *powerful*, and that I have the ability to respond to what it needs. I can slow down when I'm out of breath; I can pump my legs harder when I want to really work up a sweat. Even when my legs hurt, even when my lungs burn, even when the heat gets unbearable, running makes me *feel*, and feeling reminds me that this body is mine, this body is mine, this body is mine.

Is everything okay now?
Of course not. What a silly question. If you're holding out for *everything* to be okay, I think you're just setting yourself up to be disappointed. But I like to think that even if I wasn't a rape survivor, then everything still wouldn't be okay. But there are days when everything feels okay. And increasingly, there are more and more days when *I* am okay. And that's a start.

At twelve, you found your answer in a book. Have you stumbled upon other helpful titles?
The Gift, a collection of poetry by Hafiz, translated by Daniel Ladinsky. I wish I had had this book as a high schooler, but I only just discovered it this week, as a matter of fact. It's such an invaluable little gem of a poetry collection. It has reminded me so much about the beauty that is everywhere, both within and beyond ourselves. The hardest part of recovery for me is reminding myself I am worthy, and this book sends that message loud and clear on every single page.

JANE TODAY

Jane Cochrane is a poet and journalist. Originally from North Carolina, she recently graduated from college in Los Angeles with a degree in creative writing. She now lives in New York City.

PINBALL
By G. DONALD CRIBBS

Pull back and bang—this round arcs,
Hammers mind against bumpers:
Bah-ling-da-ding-ding-ding!
Flashes of flesh, movement rip-
ping its way through, havoc of
Thoughts too dark to speak.

Playing with yourself again, I see?
Questions bring up a flood of shame.
Staccato reply to shrug it off: *Everything is fine, and you?*
I deflect shiny metal balls as they
Ricochet, blades across my insides,
Where bleeding hides, staunched
By long-buried shards, images

Of everything he did to me. What was
Taken rises from deep places. Bile divots,
Drops target, and I'm back there again,
When it happened, fah-whip da-dingding!
Flipper bats scrambling to contain
Every ball careening down the lanes.

Hands on my hip, his mouth whispers near my ear: *I'm up next.*

Now it's on overdrive, balls fire from
All sides, ba-ding-ding, one slingshots,
Da-ding, another through the spinner,
The squish of sweat, his haste, panic trips
Rollover switches, ba-da-bada-ding!
Coming in fast, each flash fires

Across lamps in the lane, with no apron to stop
As he grinds himself against me: *Let's play another round.*

DONALD UNFILTERED
ON RESILIENCE

Don, what does this poem mean to you?
For me, this poem captures what it is like as a sexual abuse survivor to relive the trauma, or experience a flashback, or an unwanted memory that sucker punches me in the gut and leaves me splayed on the ground in a fetal position, gasping. This year, it has been forty years since my abuse first occurred, but even so, my abuser can still creep his way into my thoughts and consume me, if I let him, and that both terrifies me and makes me incredibly angry at the same time. I have to work very hard not to let him back in, but there are times when I have another nightmare, or experience sleep paralysis, and it's not always easy to keep him at arm's length. Sometimes, he gets in anyway. When that happens, I try to lean in, to literally lean forward into the sucker punch, and make myself go through it, so I can get something positive out of it, and find a way to heal just a little more despite what triggered me in the first place. By choosing to remain present, I regain my dignity and find a way to better myself, rather than allow him to abuse me all over again.

Since the poem reflects on a trigger, can you tell us briefly what happened?
When I was four, I was sexually abused by my stepfather. He also sexually abused my sibling, but I didn't know this at the time because my abuser lied and told me he wouldn't hurt my brother and my sister if I cooperated with him.

Who was the first person you told? Did that person listen to you?
I told my mother after my siblings and I realized two of the three of us were being sexually abused. My sibling's story is not mine to tell, so I'm remaining respectfully vague here. My abuser's grooming language is what tipped us off. He had lied and told each of us that if we cooperated with him, he would spare our siblings. We thought we were sparing each other through our compliance. Once we realized we were taking the bullet for nothing, we told our mother. I am thankful my mother believed me. I don't know how I would have recovered if she hadn't.

It's heartening when adult allies show up. After you told your mother, did you report the crime?
Yes, and a warrant was issued for his arrest with the charge of sodomy. I was four at the time of my sexual abuse, which lasted about six months. As an adult, this still stuns me when I reflect that I had the tenacity as a four-year-old to face such a difficult choice. I'm glad I reported the crime, but I wish my voice and my rights were better protected and justice had been better served.

Can you bring us through that a little?
My abuser was charged with sodomy, but the process was dragged out over two years. Initially, my abuser denied the charges and claimed his innocence. After a year and a half, he confessed to the crime of aggravated sexual assault—due to the quantity of occurrences and my age at the time of the abuse—and his lawyer walked out on him. A few months later he was charged and put in prison, but his sentence was reduced because my testimony was thrown out.

The law of the state I lived in required that we not be in the same state as our abuser during the litigation, trial, and sentencing. Once he was put in prison, we were allowed to return to the state where we had been living. We lived with our grandparents during that interim time and traveled back (across country) by train several times to meet with social workers, the judge, the lawyers, and the related, pretrial aspects of the case.

I remember going into judge's chambers and recounting all the occurrences, exactly what happened with each one, where they happened, and who was there. I was able to share these details with the judge, despite my age, but I was unprepared when they decided to test whether I could do the same in court in front of my abuser. They briefly told me I was safe, but I didn't believe them, especially when they brought him into judge's chambers. He was cuffed—hands and feet—and wearing an orange jumpsuit. I recall he was fuming mad, growling his words, directing his anger and his threats at me, saying he would kill me, and I recall my reaction: I froze. I couldn't say a word with him in the room, and I didn't trust the adults there to keep him away from me.

Instead, the adults decided things for me. They decided I was too young to handle it, but they made no efforts to assure me then and there that I was safe, nor did they read my nonverbal cues and realize I was having a flight reaction. In that moment, I had dissociated without realizing it. They failed to support me the way I needed to be supported. I wasn't afforded the choice on my own to decide if I was able to handle it. Frankly, if I was able to handle the abuse, I was certainly able to handle the challenge to face my abuser in court and have the right to use my voice to see justice served. I had evidenced this by speaking openly with the judge prior to them bringing my abuser in. They made the wrong call. He was sentenced based fully on my sibling's testimony, but with a record that another minor had also been abused. It wasn't until nearly forty years later that I would recover my voice and publish my first novel, which is a fictionalized version of my own sexual abuse experience. That moment is where I reclaimed my voice, the one that had been taken from me by my abuser—since silence is an aspect brought about by the shame inherent with sexual abuse. In addition, my voice had been taken by the adults who decided my testimony would be thrown out. They had heard me detail exactly what had been done to me, yet I was not afforded the dignity of reclaiming my voice, which I eventually learned was an essential part of my recovery. Fortunately, I found my own way to take my voice back, and for that, I am grateful.

So, what happened next?
In some ways, justice was served, but in many ways, it was not. My abuser was arrested, charged, and sentenced for some of his crimes. I wish he had faced the full brunt of his actions and the consequences of what he did to us. Unfortunately, he was not. His sentence was for seven years. I think he got out on "good behavior." I have not seen or heard from him since, and I have no idea of his whereabouts. I have looked online to see if anything has surfaced, out of concern for future victims, but I have not found any information about that. Instead, I wrote a book and have completed a master's degree program to become a clinical mental health counselor to help survivors more fully recover from the aftermath of their abuse. Currently, I am a full-time counselor for clients coming out of drug and alcohol dependence and addiction. Many survivors

self-medicate to alleviate the pain of their trauma and sexual abuse. This was not my experience, but I can certainly empathize with my clients and their choice to self-medicate. Counseling is joining my client where they are and co-journeying with them through the initial stages of their healing and recovery, if they decide to extend the privilege. It's a choice. It's their choice, not mine, and I'm okay with that. I have learned how to use my voice to take back what was stolen from me. I intend to take back all that was taken multiplied times seven.

How was your personal experience in counseling? Did you have any particularly positive or negative experiences that impacted your own decision to pursue clinical mental health counseling?
I did not have a positive experience in counseling, especially the initial years of counseling following the abuse. It was a kind of unraveling. I moved a lot growing up. I moved more than fifty times before I turned eighteen. With each move, the counseling followed like this dark shadow I dragged behind me. Sometimes, the counselor changed, and I'd have to start all over again. That became exhausting. It's hard enough to extend myself to trust another human being, but a counselor who wanted me to fling open all the drapes and closed doors and secrets from my childhood was a whole new level of stretching and trusting. Many times, it hurt.

I think somewhere along the way, I figured out for myself that I had believed a lie my whole life: I didn't matter. I was unwanted. Unloved. Other people were wanted, were loved. Other people mattered, not me. I felt damaged and broken and beyond repair. I was ashamed of myself, for my participation in my abuse. A secondary lie I came to believe: Don't ask for help, just figure it out on my own. I don't know that I gained these insights through the counseling process because so many times the adults made assumptions about me, and when that message came through in the session, I died a little, and I retreated to a back hallway place within myself where I stopped trying with that counselor. Instead, I waited. I knew there'd be another one, and I'd try again, but mostly, I had to do the hard work on my own. That was a lonely place. I cried so many tears.

There were times in counseling where the counselors did some of the same things my abuser did to groom me for abuse. When that happened, I knew I couldn't trust them. A part of me hated counselors growing up. So, coming full circle to where I'm at now, as an adult, it's ironic that I have become what I hated. This choice was no accident. I purposely entered this program because I knew what it had been like growing up, and I knew better than most why it hadn't been helpful to me. Having walked through my own recovery journey, I know what worked for me and a lot of what didn't. I decided I could be the person I never had, as a counselor, and I would find a way to be the listening ear, one who had walked through my own fire and found a way through the flames.

Given your experience, do you think our law enforcement is effective in dealing with rape and sexual assault?

First responders, including law enforcement, social workers, counselors, psychologists, medical personnel, and others—those who are on the front lines with survivors of sexual assault, rape, or abuse—need to understand what it's like for survivors and receive at least basic training to better support us. Minimal training should include how triggers work, survival skills such as flight—dissociation, numbing/freeze responses to trauma—and intrusive memories, flashbacks, or memories of the abuse or assault. Trauma and abuse survivors often have trouble orienting themselves to time because of the way that traumatic memory stores itself in the mind. When recalled or retrieved, those memories feel very much like they are being experienced for the first time, despite the individual's knowledge that it is a traumatic memory. Thus, sorting through those memories and making sense of them is hard to conceptualize for the trauma survivor. They are often flooded with sensory memories of how things looked, felt, smelled, or sounded. It's like a horrible movie you can't shut off or block out. It's a living nightmare.

A survivor may not be able to trust others to protect them. Those who work directly with survivors should be aware of this fact and seek ways to better support survivors. I recall being asked by adults at the age of four to tell details of everything that happened. This was very triggering for me, and those same adults offered me candy bars and soda as incentives to comply with their requests. The problem was, this was also the grooming tactic used by my abuser.

Those who work with survivors should know what grooming techniques are as well as terms such as gas lighting—where an abuser tells a victim of abuse that what they just saw, heard, or experienced is not true, and then rewrites or retells them what they saw, heard, experienced, or felt.

Today, there seems to be a growing awareness about triggers, such as with the appearance of "trigger warnings." However, opinions are mixed about these. As someone who has experience with PTSD, counseling, and trauma, what is your opinion of trigger warnings?

Triggers are some of the hardest aspects of recovery because a smell, a touch, a word, or a turn of phrase that brings a flashback to the surface can become overwhelming in an instant. You're going about your own business, and *boom:* There it is. Again. Pounding away like waves at the shore. Only the ocean is all of your memories drowning you under their weight, and you get pulled under, desperate to find air so you can catch your breath.

I personally appreciate those who take the time to post a trigger warning, since then I get to decide if I'm up for the fight or if today, no, I'm not. It gives me the space to catch myself, back away, and set it aside until later when I am ready. I posted a trigger warning at the front of my own novel, *The Packing House.* I would advise all of those who write, speak, or share in this realm to tread softly and to consider the needs of those in recovery above our own. The reason? Because we don't know what stage that person is at, and they could be working through some especially vulnerable places and need the warning as a way to protect themselves from further harm.

An excellent source to delve into what it's like for someone suffering from PTSD is Dr. Bessel van der Kolk's seminal work for the trauma survivor, *The Body Keeps the Score: Brain, Mind, and Body in the Healing of Trauma.* In addition, it's important to note that there is more than the diagnosis of PTSD. There are other options related to recovery and healing that include resiliency and wellness, and these may be better explained through posttraumatic growth (PTG), rather than PTSD. There are also other degrees of posttraumatic stress, such as posttraumatic stress symptoms (PTSS). But most of all, find your own way to climb out of the dark cellar of your abuse, and find your own pathway to recovery and healing that feels right for you. You are the most important piece to your recovery. You. As a suggestion for a starting point, I point at the grass. Watch what it does when it gets crushed beneath our footsteps: It bounces back. Be the grass. Bounce back. Keep getting back up. Never stop.

DONALD TODAY

G. Donald Cribbs has written and published poetry and short stories since high school. Donald is a graduate of Messiah College in English and education, and he is a nationally certified counselor. He and his wife and four boys reside in central Pennsylvania, where the author is hard at work on his next book, the sequel to his debut novel, *The Packing House* (Booktrope, 2016). Having lived and traveled abroad in England, France, Belgium, Germany, China, and Thailand (you can guess where he lived and where he visited), the author loves languages and how they connect us all. Coffee and Nutella are a close second.

DEAR DIARY
By MAYA DEMRI

Dear diary,
I'm six years old and I started school, but I hate it. All the kids are so mean to me. It hurts my feelings so much. I just want to have friends to play with. I feel lonely all the time. My older sister doesn't like me anymore. She is a teenager and all she cares about is *her* friends. What about me? We used to be best friends.

Dear diary,
Something really weird happened today. My boy cousin said, "Show me yours, and I will show you mine." I didn't understand it, and I had no idea why he asked me to take off my underwear. Nobody ever asked me that before. I felt so uncomfortable. I didn't know what to say, so I did what he asked. He said he will play with me. I just didn't want to be alone.
     I'm always alone.

Dear diary,
I'm in second grade now. Today, a kid pushed me into a cactus plant in the school garden, and I came home bleeding with needles stuck in my skin. I don't know why he did it. All I remember is that I was walking near the garden at recess, and suddenly this kid from a different class came behind me and shoved me into the cactus plant. I was crying on the ground in between the plants, and I was bleeding from my elbow and from all the other needles pierced in my skin. But it is my heart that hurts. I just want to be loved. Soon after, one of the teachers noticed and took me to the school nurse. My mom came and brought me home, where I spent the rest of my day crying, and now, writing to you, dear diary—you are my only friend.

Hi, diary,
So, today really sucked! My class teacher had a long discussion about my bullying situation. I didn't say a thing. It was so

embarrassing to have a whole hour just about me being the school freak. I hate this school. I do love my class teacher because she is nice, and when she hugs me, I feel safe. I wouldn't mind going to school if she was the only one there. I am going to tell Mom I am sick tomorrow. I learned from my big sister how to fake a fever. She just drank hot water, then measured her temperature and showed the thermometer to Mom! That's what I'm gonna do. It looks easy.

Dear diary,
I turned nine last week and my mom threw a party just for the family. All the extended family came. It wasn't so much fun because my boy cousin, who was also invited, is really starting to bother me. He touches me all the time and makes me feel so yucky. I told him I don't want him to lick me and all the other gross stuff he does—and forces me to do. I can't even tell *you*, dear diary, and you are my best and only friend. I feel disgusting. I hate my body now. I just want to wash my hands over and over and over again. I can't stop. I feel like a trash can that can never be emptied. I wish I could just take off my skin and ask God to give me a new clean skin. I don't know what is happening. What is this? I don't know what to do. He is here all the time now, and he sleeps over a lot. I wish he would just go away and never come back. I'd rather be alone.

Dear diary,
I'm in third grade now. Going to school is still a nightmare. I don't have any friends, and I am so sick of being called "cry baby" or "ugly." All the kids call me "stupid" because I can't get good grades even though I study so hard. I can't concentrate in class because sometimes I feel dead, and I forget that I'm alive, so I stop listening. The teacher is talking, but I can't hear or remember anything she says. It's as if I am not even there. Maybe I am stupid? Right after my mom picked me up from my tutor, they talked about dyslexia, and I got really upset. I said, "NO! I don't want some paper to confirm that I am retarded." I started to cry, and I left, slamming the door behind me. I didn't care that I was rude because it's bad enough the kids call me stupid, but my mom and tutor, too?

Dear diary,
The summer is starting and I am about to finish third grade. I was in the pool today at my grandparents (Pepe and Meme). I love them so much. It's fun diving in the water and pretending I am a mermaid or a fairy. I wish I was one for real, and that I could just fly away to a magical place where everybody loves me and treats me well. I had so much fun until "that" cousin and my other two male cousins came in the pool. Then, when nobody noticed, they started pressing their bodies against me, taking turns. I couldn't speak. It was like I was dead and they were alive, hurting me. Nobody paid attention to what they were doing. They made it look as if they were playing with me or lifting me up, but I could feel their "thing" pressing against mine. It felt bad and I know what they were doing. He must have told them they could do this. I hate this and I hate him. Even the water in the pool can't wash away this yucky feeling.

Dear diary,
I had the most awful school day ever! At recess, one of the kids took the pencil bag of one of the most violent kids in my grade (Ben), and put it in my backpack while I was outside of the classroom. When I came back, all the things that were in my bag were on the floor. Ben looked at me with evil eyes, and I ran to the hallway. Then he cornered me to the wall and got really close to my body, and he just started hitting and kicking me. So many tears fell down my face. I felt really unsafe because he was pressing his body on top of me, which reminded me of what my cousins do to me. After Ben was done kicking me, he left. I stayed crying on the floor. I hate my life—and this school. I am going to ask Mom to transfer me to a different school next year when I will be in fourth grade.

Hi, diary,
You are really the only one that listens to me. I turned ten years old last month, and I thought growing older would make life easier, but it's not. My older sister still hates me. She hits me and tells me horrible things just like those kids in school. From all the painful things she says, what hurts me the most is when she says she wishes I was dead. I don't know why she hates me so much. She says I am the center of attention because I have troubles in school. As if it is

my fault. My parents keep fighting a lot, and I don't know if it's my fault. They scream so loud at each other. Me and my older sister listen to them through the wall, and every time there is a moment of silence, we both fear that one of them may have killed the other.

I switched elementary schools this year, and it doesn't seem to be working out. The kids call me fat. I can't even look at myself anymore in jazz class. I hate my reflection! And I hate who I am! I am so ugly. I bet if I was pretty, I would have lots of friends and nobody would hurt me. I wish someone would just love me. I enjoy company and playing. Every day, I walk into class, all the kids are laughing and talking with each other, but I am always alone. I'm never invited to slumber or birthday parties, and it hurts. I just want friends. I feel as if I am the only person left in the world. I wish so much to be in the cool kids' group. I am not even in the "nerd" group. I belong nowhere.

Dear diary,
Turning eleven didn't make things better either. This "monster cousin" is always here. He has been sleeping at our house for two months now. I am scared! Every time I see him I can't breathe because I know what is going to happen, and no one protects me from him or from my older sister, who is becoming meaner and meaner day by day. I am not doing anything to her. I want to die sometimes. I dream about what it is like in heaven. Are pretty butterflies there? Can I fly? I always wanted to fly. Last weekend at Grandma's, he took me into her room, locked the door, but also put the futon bed at the door. He licked me and forced me to do the same to him. Then he did the same at my parents' house this week when he stayed over. It was the worst night of my life! He dragged me out of my room at one a.m. and locked me in the attic. Then he lied on top of me after he pushed me on my parent's old mattress. I couldn't breathe. He always puts sheets over my face. It's like being in hell and not being able to see anything. I feel dead. Maybe I am? I don't understand anything anymore. I just want to cry. I will write you more tomorrow. I can't stop crying. . . .

Dear diary,
I cried myself to sleep last night. I want to tell you all that happened

because I can't tell anyone else. I mean . . . sometimes I do want to tell my teacher, but I can't. I am so ashamed. She will probably think I am disgusting. My "cousin from hell"—-that's what I call him now—said that if I tell anyone what happened, people will think I am a "whore." This word! What if I am a whore? I don't want this, God. I don't want any of this. Last night, what I didn't tell you was . . . okay, it's kind of hard to say. . . . After he got on me, he . . . I think he raped me. I am so scared. What if one day he will get me pregnant? I know I don't have my period yet, but I am eleven. I heard girls can't get it young. Dear diary, if that ever happens I don't know what I'll do. . . . That was not the worst of that night, though. He placed me like I was just his toy, a nobody with no soul, as if I don't feel when he hurts me. He never even talks to me. He just does whatever he wants. Licks me as if I was food. He put stuff inside of me, and I couldn't walk after. I couldn't pee all night, and it hurts between my legs all the time now. After he finished at six a.m., he just left. I stayed there crying and confused, but then I got up and went to the bathroom in the attic. I washed my hands for half an hour, and I still don't feel clean. Then I started taking little bites of the soap. I didn't care if it was gonna poison me. I felt so disgusting, I just wanted to be clean.

Dear diary,
I know it's weird, but I feel as if kids in school know about what's going on with "my cousin from hell." I feel different. I am not like everybody anymore, and I think they know that. After all that he did, I feel like an alien. That's what the "cousin from hell" made of me, and now they know "I am bad." I am almost twelve. That means that I am almost an adult, so I decided to start a crash diet. I read all about it in a magazine. The woman on the cover looks happy and thin. I want to be so skinny nobody will ever call me fat. I will be popular and everybody will love me.

Dear diary,
I am having a really hard time. My parents are mad because I don't want to eat. I lost forty pounds this summer, but I needed to. I am just going to lose a little more, and I will stop. My parents took me to see so many therapists, but I don't like any of them. I feel threatened,

and I don't want to tell them anything. I don't want anyone to control *my* body. It belongs only to me. I started junior high last week. I got accepted into an art school. It's better here, but the kids still mock me, sometimes. It could be worse. I love painting. There are crazy rumors about me all over the city, though. Kids from my old school are telling everybody that the only reason that I lost all this weight is because I "had a surgery." That is crazy!! Do they really think my parents will pay for that, or even agree to it? I am so happy to be out of that school.

Dear diary,
Something *amazing* happened last week. Maybe because I just turned fourteen. It started bad when my "cousin from hell" trapped me in my grandma's room again. He pushed me to the wall and started to touch me. I couldn't breathe. I was so scared that I felt as if the tears in my eyes froze and couldn't even slide out of my eyes, but then I suddenly woke up. It was as if God put life in me again and made me able to fight him. I pushed him with my hands, and I kicked him right between his legs. He released his grip, and I ran out of the room and out of the house.

    I looked at the sky. It was dark, and I prayed to God and asked him to stop this nightmare. I begged my divine father to make him stop hurting me. The following day, the girls in my school started to make fun of me in the bathroom, but the weirdest thing happened—I stood up for myself. I told them nobody will undermine me ever again and that I will not take this anymore. You should have seen their faces. I was so proud of myself. Since then, nobody has bothered me in school. They respect me now. I even made some new friends in the art department. It feels so great to finally belong somewhere. Anna is really nice and she likes sports as much as I do. When we don't paint in class, we run together at the school's field during recess.

Dear diary,
I am sixteen years old now. I am sorry I didn't write you for a while. I was in the children's hospital for the past three months because I was barely eating, and I was making myself throw up, too. I almost died a few times when my heartbeat went too low. It was really scary and I realized I want to LIVE.

Since I got back I refuse to go to family events my "cousin from hell" attends, and I leave the house if he comes to our place. He can't hurt me anymore, and I don't want to hurt myself either—LIFE IS GOOD.

————————————

MAYA UNFILTERED

I AM FREE

This piece shows you slowly realizing that something was wrong and only later naming what your cousin did as rape. How did your understanding unfold?

As a kid I didn't understand what was happening. I had no words for it, and I didn't know that I was being abused. No adult ever taught me that someone touching me against my will is wrong. I was a shy, sensitive girl, and I was scared. When I was about ten years old, I started to understand that what he did was not normal and that with time the molestation became rape. I felt trapped and terrified because my abuser threatened me that if I told, then everybody would think I was "a whore."

The weight of that word kept me quiet for years, until I started high school and girls were talking about virginity. They asked me if I was a virgin. I said yes, but in my heart something told me no. I finally remembered all that happened, and everything I had buried in my bubble of denial; however, I didn't yet tell anyone. I wasn't ready. No therapist who worked with me on the eating disorder ever asked me if anything happened, so I didn't say anything. But a year later I started acting classes, and I had a breakdown as I was standing near my teacher playing a scene. I suddenly felt so unsafe. I had a flashback, and I told her. My acting teacher spoke to my mom and suggested I see a psychologist, but my mom didn't know how to deal with the truth, nor did anyone else in my family. I felt alone, and I had no support, but when I moved out of my parents' home and started college, I was able to finally start my healing journey. After many trials with different therapists, I finally found the right people: professionals and friends who helped me by validating my abuse and wrapping me with safe hugs. Thanks to support from female friends I call sisters, my emotional mom Dana, my rabbi Jill, and other teachers and friends, I came to fully understand that I had been abused, that it was wrong, and that I deserve better.

It's great that you were able to find emotional support and feel healed in some ways, but did you ever consider justice or pursue reporting the crime?

I did not report the crime because my sexual abuse happened within the family, which made things much more complicated when it came to getting justice. I was worried about my ability to handle the stress of a trial, as I was already struggling with anorexia, and I didn't want to risk the possibility of my medical and mental health getting worse. I thought nobody would believe me, probably because no one from my family supported me about getting justice, not to mention the many members in my family who called me a liar and a witch. Not getting justice hurt and delayed my recovery; however, when I became an activist and founded my organization Peace Again, I found new ways to give myself justice through my own healing and through the opportunity to help others.

Anorexia plays a big part in this story. Do you think that the anorexia was a direct result of the abuse or something unrelated?

Being sexually abused and controlled by another being made me feel a complete lack of control over my body, and dieting made me feel strong, like I had authority over my body again. Now that I remember what happened to me, I know that I developed anorexia only as a result of the abuse. However, I learned to love and forgive myself for something that is not my fault, and I became my own best friend—something I never thought possible for me.

Do you ever think of what you might say to those classmates who bullied you? About what they didn't understand or how they could have been allies instead of antagonists?

Kids can be very mean. The younger they are, the harder it is for them to process and deal with struggles. While I do believe that many kids who bully might suffer some kind of abuse themselves—

and would maybe relate to another peer they are actually bullying who might suffer the same abuse as them—I do not believe kids at an age younger than eleven or twelve are able to mentally or emotionally understand the effects of abuse or loss that could be the cause of their aggressive behavior and bullying of others. Therefore, I do not believe there was anything different I could have done or said to stop the abuse in school.

I accept my past and know what didn't break me definitely made me stronger.

You take power back at the end of your story. You find your voice and tell the bullies to stop. You take power back by distancing yourself from the perpetrator. Do you ever think about what you might say to him if you were to speak to him today, from this place of empowerment?
If I could talk to my abuser now, I would tell him, "You're pathetic and sick. You don't have any power over me anymore. I am a free, strong young woman, and I'm going to achieve anything I want in my life. You don't exist in it anymore. The people who betrayed me don't exist in it, either. Good-bye!"

MAYA TODAY

Maya Demri is *not* an illusion; she is the *real* thing. She started her artistic life at age four when she found the magic of ballet and the freedom in painting. Over the years she studied visual arts, dance, acting, and singing professionally. In college she discovered her soul's talent of writing and became an author as well. She believes that arts can truly heal and awaken humanity's consciousness. Activism is her biggest passion, and she is happy to dedicate her life to help protect the rights of those who are not heard and assist with their healing.

WHERE I GO WHEN I GO AWAY
By AALUK EDWARDSON

He's in the room before me,
filling up so much space.

My fingers grip the blankets.
My legs, too short to touch the ground.

I fear that all is falling.
All of a sudden,
I've become a frozen little girl.

My body—stuck—remembers: pain from before.

I can't see the man above me.
I can't see his larger shape.

Am I really here again?

I know it's coming soon.
He'll pierce me, fast and strong
in the place I hold most dear.

He moves in closer, knowing
I may try to jump off the bed.

Like a deer, I'm stuck,
small again and blinded,
not by lights but fear.

Should I try to jump, now?

Too late, he's too close now, too near.
With his stronger hands, he pushes me
and forces me to lay.

I squirm deeper into the bed
trying to disappear.

I know what's in his hand.
I close my mouth,
trying to keep it out.

With his elbow on my chest, he pins me to the bed.
Squeezing my cheeks with his hands
he forces
liquid down my throat.

I'm coughing, coughing, syrup.
Now I know I'm in quicksand.

Within a moment I'm drowsy,
not strong enough to stand.

He reaches down below.
Not big enough to kick.

Ripping me open, he stabs me

in all of me—it hurts.

With each piercing stroke,
he cuts me in my most deep.

Sharp pain penetrates my whole body.
It shoots out from my root.

With each painful thrust of his penis,
he slashes me, again, and again, and again.

I have no control of anything, I can't make it stop.
Pain inflicted in the place from which we all connect,
the place we come from, the place we knew
before we knew fear.

Before him I was light. I held joy so easily there.

What he did was conquer.
He conditioned me to think
that my body was not my own.

Is this pain, real?
Is this pain, life?
Is this distraction, a memory?
Is this distraction, life?

Rhythmically, he told me
with each thrust he screamed so loud
that I am not beloved
that the world is a prison
where I only experience unending pain.

Over time, I learned one thing I could do.

I could leave my body entirely,
let him have it all.

And through my mind, disappear
to a quiet place that's static
and timeless.
Somewhere good for deer . . .

It's not a place of joy, but there I'm so numb
that I don't feel fear.

This is where I go, even now that I am big
a part of me is always here.

. . . *Aaluk?*

I feel like I've been sitting,
like I'm on the edge of a chair,

like I've been caught
in a frozen and empty stare.

I blink.

I think I see my face.
I think I see a mirror.

In a moment, I am crying.
Because, in this moment, I can feel.

Aaluk, are you here?

I feel something stir from deep inside me,
Aaluk, am I where?

. . .

Almost like a movie, maybe it's a memory.
Something I've denied all these years.

I'm coming back to life now, I'm big and grown and looking
in my bathroom mirror.

I'm looking through my eyes,
deep into that frozen and empty stare.

Coming to, I realize
I've been frozen, stuck and crying,
lost in that memory of seemingly unending fear.

The man who was once above me
whose shape was never clear
is gone, now again,

but for the first time since he hurt me,
I see myself.
I'm *here*.

Seeing myself, I recognize, through this dirty mirror,
the part of me forgotten and left alone for all those years.

Aaluk, I am here.

I see a tiny me, forgotten,
lying naked on a bare and dirty floor.

This is my deepest part, my broken little deer,
the part I locked away who holds so much fear.

I cry and cry as I realize
how truly alone she has been.

I'm so sorry, I'm so very sorry,
I'm sorry I left, I'm so sorry I left you *here.*

I thought I was protecting you—shutting you away from the pain.

But I forgot you in this lonely place
with no light or love to hold you.

Only darkness and fear.

I don't remember light.
But now, you are here.
I'd forgotten there was anything else
but this room, this floor, this fear.

With a deep breath I see you rest.
I see me letting go for the first time
in twenty years.

Holding you, I realize, I have to grow you up
because you are still so little.
I see your gashes, where he slashed you
all over your broken body.

I used to think that triggers
were always only bad.
I felt lost to their effects,
freezing me in moments
I wanted to forget I'd ever had.

But now I see behind them is where you've always been.

Seeing you there so helpless, I remember how hurt I felt.

Now I will be your mother. I will hold you close.
Cradling you so gently, know that I am here.

I will listen to your voice.
I will rock away your pain.

I see you now, so fully.

Both the pain,
and beauty,
in your little loving face.

I realize, it's through healing *you*
I can heal me.
I can heal us.

It's through learning from this pain
that I'll finally find that happy place
that I've heard about
but never thought I could attain.

Standing up, I have you.
My feet are firmly on *this ground*.

And now I bring you back,
the road in healing, long.
But together we are safe.
Together, we are strong.

UNFREEZING

Your poem is about being triggered into remembering sexual abuse.
Would you mind sharing more about the abuse you experienced?
I am very open to talking about it. I think sharing experiences of
abuse in a nonexploitative way is not only healing for the person
who was abused but can help educate others who weren't abused in
ways that might help abuse from occurring in the first place. I was
repeated sexually abused as a child. It started when I very young,
first through interactions with a young male babysitter, then by two
family members: an uncle and an older cousin. It was all over by
the time I was six. I always knew, deep down, that something had
happened, but it wasn't until I was an adult and away from home that
I was able to face what had happened. I didn't know it, but for most
of my life, words, sounds, stories, movies, almost anything connected
to what happened could violently trigger me into feeling abused. But
because I hadn't admitted to myself that I had been abused, I didn't
know I was being triggered. I thought there was something wrong
with me. I didn't understand why I'd get so quickly angry or suddenly
feel so deeply hurt. What I felt was acutely rooted in my body, and so
I thought there was something wrong with how I was put together. I
thought I was broken. It wasn't until I started to face what happened,
as an adult, that I was able to stop blaming myself and begin to heal.
Recognizing what triggered me and how I was triggered was the first
step in healing from what happened to me as a child.

What prompted you to realize and face the trauma?
The birth of my son caused me to look at my body in different ways.
Before him, I hated my body. For as long as I could remember, I
felt very uncomfortable physically and didn't feel a close identity
with the body I lived in. My daily experience often mirrored the
disassociation I reference in the poem: I felt cold, disconnected,
and like I was observing my life from a distant, faraway vantage
point. But, to me, being a mother meant I had to be more present,
physically. He needed me to care for him with my body—through
feeding him, holding him, and loving him. I wanted more than

anything for him to feel loved. Because of this, I began for the first time to see my body as strong and capable of showing deep and profound love. And I loved this because I loved him.

I remember, when my son was six months old, having a significant conversation with my older sister, Rachel. After sharing with her some unusual and recurring dreams I'd been having, she gently broached the subject of sexual abuse. She and my mother had asked me if I'd experienced sexual abuse before, but it wasn't until after I had my son that I was able to honestly face anything. Until that point I couldn't remember anything. Memories before eight years old were few and far between, and very fuzzy. After I had my son, something inside me began to stir. I started having nightmares that felt familiar, but I couldn't remember ever having them before. In the dreams, I was very young, a baby or a toddler, lying in a bed paralyzed in fear. I could sense someone coming toward me, but I couldn't move. Not my hands, not my legs, not my neck, not anything. I felt so much fear, it was crippling. I would try to squirm or try to wake myself up, but whatever I tried, I stayed motionless, and whoever was coming toward me got closer and closer. My sister let me share these dreams, these horrors I couldn't escape at night, and listened. When I shared them with her, I could feel the warmth of her heart as I looked into her eyes. It was in connecting with her heart that I was able to share these fears and feel through them to reach a better understanding. By example, she taught me to listen to people with an open heart. In sharing these dreams, she let me say what I couldn't say, and in doing so, she helped me start to heal.

In my poem, the other voice is the voice of the little girl I was as I was being abused, and it's the voice of my older sister who first taught me how to listen and speak from an open heart that can hold both love and pain. This is what I needed to begin to heal. I needed to welcome the little girl I had hidden away to protect—but kept at bay because I was scared—back into my heart.

What do you wish someone had said to you during your recovery?
I don't wish I was told anything in particular, but I do wish we lived in a society that was more willing and able to hear experiences of both love and pain. People love listening to the joy and triumph of recovery, but we also need people to listen to the less "pretty" things.

I'd like to see more people hold space to listen to the pain and fear involved in recovery. We often need others to hear our pain, our sadness, and our fear because we can't hold it all ourselves. And we shouldn't. Pain, fear, and sadness are not meant to be held but let go, and it's easier to do this if you know someone is listening with an open heart.

People often argue about whether rape culture exists in America. Do you think it exists, and would silence around the topic of sexual violence also be considered a symptom of rape culture?
The idea that rape culture doesn't exist in America is wrong. Rape culture includes ways of thinking that perpetuate and normalize rape. A rape culture denier might think that people who are married can't rape each other and that clothing choices cause sexual assault. These perspectives are based in denial. But they don't work. Denying rape culture doesn't take away from the fact that America does have a problem with how sexual assault—in our homes, in our schools, in our churches, and in public, anywhere—is or isn't acknowledged and addressed. What denial really signifies is fear—fear in facing the truth that lies behind it.

One interesting part of your poem is when you talk about triggers as part of the healing process. Can you talk a little bit more about that?
The most holistic and effective way I've learned to heal from trauma is to learn how I am triggered, whether the associated feeling is pain, loss, fear, sadness, or anger. Because it is in facing these triggers that I see how and why I am affected by the world around me. Facing feelings like this is hard because you have to practice self-compassion. If I can learn from how I am triggered and work on neutralizing how a trigger affects me, over time I become less affected. I don't feel like I am broken anymore because I understand why I have responded, and in some cases still respond, to certain triggers. Life is much less overwhelming because I have worked on neutralizing triggers.

When I first started facing the things that triggered me, I responded with either paralyzing fear or deep sadness. I felt like the scared little girl I was when I was being abused. In recognizing the trigger, I was able to begin to see that little girl instead of become her. As a little girl, I didn't have the emotional or intellectual ability or capacity to respond to the complex emotions the abuse incurred. Standing witness to myself experiencing these difficult emotions made it so I didn't have to be a little girl. I could take care of myself as a little girl in a way I didn't know how to do then, but I can as an adult. I learned to listen to what I needed while I was triggered and what I needed to feel safe and loved afterward. In the beginning, I saw a very little girl and learned to give her very basic things like sleep, nourishing food, space to cry and be held. As I've grown in my relationship to myself when I am triggered, what I've needed has also changed. Sometimes I need a bath. Sometimes I need to run. Sometimes I need to call my best friend. Sometimes I need a banana, because I love bananas.

What would you like to say to a teen or kid in your situation?
Be kind to yourself. Listen to your deepest self, the first you anyone ever knew. The you that comes from the unity of all things. The you made of pure light and energy. The you that loves and laughs, hopes and dreams. Because it's that *you* you need right now. And remember, it's that you that survives, no matter what. It's that you that's unbreakable. It's your spirit. Your light.

Sometimes it feels like people can take light away from us. Can break our spirits, can bend our minds to make us think we are dirty, we are bad and we deserve to be hurt. But those are all lies, denials of the truth. You are brilliantly strong and timelessly beautiful. Tap into that stream, that well, the water of your spirit that forever flows from the opposite of fear, love.

AALUK TODAY

Aaluk Edwardson is an Alaskan Eskimo woman raised on the tundra and the shores of the Arctic Ocean. She grew up in a community where storytelling is an art still practiced, and listening to the wisdom in the natural world around you is not only intriguing, it's how you survive. She writes for spirit and purpose, listening for the music in the words the two make when they dance together. She was abused as a young girl for an extended period of time, and in falling into a rhythm in her writing that carries a voice of both spirit and purpose, she has found healing. She believes in the power of healing through art and hopes she will see the world grow more and more engaged with both, healing and art, as time passes. She has been writing since she was ten years old; her first exploration was a screenplay. She has since written songs, poems, and two plays, *Thaw* and *Coming Home*. Currently, she is working on adapting *Thaw* into a book. She has a blog (http://nomoredaggers.blogspot.com) where she shares her experiences with healing, love, hope, and light.

IN A SERIES OF SILENCES
By SHARON ABRA HANEN

They asked me (hoping I was wrong) if I knew what the word *rape* meant. It was a big word, a dangerous word, though just one syllable long.

Part of me wanted to say: *Isn't it obvious? I wouldn't have used it if I didn't think I knew what it meant. After all, I'm trying to communicate something here.* I was that kind of twelve-year-old. But the part of me that didn't know how old I was or what I was expected to know was hurt and numb and trying to shut down.

They asked me again. I just nodded. I'd said what I could.

The rest was trapped in silence.

I couldn't say more. Not in that early November evening. Not for years of days and evenings and late nights after.

I told what I had to when I had to—to the pony-tailed police officer, to the nurse with swabs and sample bags, to the counselor who spent months hoping I'd talk over ice cream. I gave scraps and shards, the fact-straight edges of what I knew, staying far away from the confused center of my feelings. Still, there was more silence than story.

I couldn't say then, or for long after, that if I'd known how I'd be hurt, not outside, not in my physical self, but inside, where my spirit and emotions lived, by being treated like a meaningless thing, I would have hid. I didn't know what was about to happen, what was happening, what would happen to who I was. If I had known, I would have blanketed myself in dry leaf drifts, pacing my breath to the breeze, protected by the tall trees that stood like strong friends.

If I could have, if I'd known I had infinite worth, as we all do, just by being, I would have flown to the tops of those pine trees pointing to the sky, above the place of *this makes no sense* and *how is this happening to me* and *I am broken, voiceless.*

If I could have, if I'd known I did not have to carry another's wounding as my own, I would have laid on the clouds and slid by the moon along to the stars.

But I could not. Not in the moments of assault. Not in coping with going back to school, wondering who might know my attacker. Not in attempts at conversation with those assigned to help me. I lost a lightness that had been true to me. My spirit was now weighed down, burdened by what I could not say, the heaviness of unsaid words straining my heart. The counselors were kind; they tried. But there was part of me that could not be reached, could not trust, could not rest, could not hope to soar. Silence held me down.

But there, in the quiet, in time, and with patience, I found a place. In some closed-off corner inside the protection, I could still feel freedom, a freedom fueled by imagination. I went back to books I had loved when I was younger, including Joan Aiken's *The Whispering Mountain,* whose adventurous healer heroine's name I borrowed as my own when my closest friends resolved to be known to each other by the names of our favorite book-character alter egos. From the safe corner of my mind filled with books, I could step into the world, do things I had enjoyed before, yet always be close to retreat, just in case.

And so I walked alert to shapes and textures and sounds that reminded me of books I'd read and books not yet written. I lost myself in music to find myself again—sitting at the piano playing improvised fragments unrecognizable to anyone else, yet somehow familiar to me, lying on the floor absorbing the strength of the bass and the poetry of the lyrics and the joy of the crowds on double and triple live-rock albums—*Frampton Comes Alive! Wings Over America*—played over and over. I laughed and cried and cooked and ran and sketched and kept alert for kindred spirits. Even though something in me was broken, I could be okay in touch with what I loved.

In time, even though there still are scars on the spirit few can see, and still at times my voice fails in disbelief or with an anxious audience, in time, I have felt safe enough to share that place with those who treat it well.

And sometimes we sit together in silence—the kind that heals, not the kind that hurts.

SUPPORT SYSTEM

Sharon, one of the things that strikes me about this piece is the
awareness and the support system of adults. That is often missing in
these stories. How did the presence of supportive adults impact you?
Because there were different professional adults involved—
policewomen, policemen, a police detective, my trauma counselor,
the hospital nurse—plus my family, I had a sense of needing and
receiving a range of support. Some were seconds or minutes, some
were months or years. Some were straightforward and practical,
some were complex and emotional. All played a role in me feeling
acknowledged, even though there was some larger force that pulled
me mostly into silence about what happened. Maybe I would
have lost myself in that silence if there hadn't been adults who, in
smaller and larger ways, let me know they heard me, believed me
as a witness to my own experience, and wanted to help, whether it
was a nurse being reassuring as I faced the rape kit, the counselor
who was available to talk over a period of months, each police
officer who tried to make it as simple for me to provide evidence as
possible. In the long term, that may have given me more of a sense
of trust in the potential for help from people who were assigned
to me by authorities than I might otherwise have had. And neither
the people in uniform nor my parents made me feel I needed to
curtail my freedom because of what happened to me, and for that
I am especially grateful. As a teen, walking, running, and biking
on my own was hugely important to me, giving me space to think
and feel and observe my world without others' filters. Solitude has
always been part of caring for my mental health, the complement to
deep friendships. As an adult, I still feel great appreciation that I'm
comfortable traveling through my day or through other parts of the
world on my own when I want to.

When it happened, who was the first person you told?
My mother, *and* I think there was someone with her—I don't
remember if it was a family friend or my father. My sense is that she
heard and understood me, and that it was the family friend who

asked if I knew what rape meant, and that my father came home later. But I could be wrong about much of that.

How did you report the crime?
My mother called the police.

So it was reported right away. Were the police part of that supportive group of adults?
My experience with law enforcement was excellent, and I was surprised at the resources available through them in our town. I had a sense of care from them, although I have wondered how much of that was related to the fact I was a child.

It's great to hear about good police response. Were charges pressed?
Charges were pressed. I'm not sure what exactly. There was a court hearing that my mother attended. I don't know much about what happened after that.

It never came up again? Were you ever curious?
I was curious at times. And I wondered a lot about what had happened to my attacker, how it had affected him. But never enough to want to open myself up to what digging into that might feel like. Until I was working on this piece—then I did try to research the case report, and I did talk to my mother about what she remembered about the legal proceedings. I was still cautious to protect my feelings—writing about the assault was already leaving some of my previously buried emotions exposed and raw.

Did you run into victim blaming in the aftermath of the assault?
I heard, in recent conversations, that at the court hearing—which I was not at—the lawyer for the attacker tried to portray me as a kind of young temptress. I was told that the impression he was trying to make was one of a girl using revealing clothing for attention. I certainly was struck by the injustice of that and also surprised in simply practical terms—what I was wearing would have been in the police records, and it happened to be the opposite of revealing: loose jean-style corduroy pants, a long-sleeved shirt, and a yellow hooded

rain slicker. From my adult perspective, it seems to me that the lawyer had very little to argue with and was grasping at straws, and ridiculous misogynistic ones at that.

That's a very clear attempt at victim blaming. Hopefully, it didn't work. Was justice served?
Traditional justice was never a concern of mine. I was concerned that no one else be hurt the same way, and that this young guy get help. He was a sixteen-year-old high school student. I don't know what happened to him or where he is now. I have wondered at times. None of my searches during the time of writing about this have turned up anything relevant.

What would you like to say to a teen or kid in your situation?
You are more valuable than anything that has ever happened to you. And I would like to give you a fragment from the thirteenth-century Persian poet Rumi:

"Let yourself be silently drawn by the strange pull of what you really love. It will not lead you astray."

It is advice I did not come across in words until I was much older, but it expresses the core of what helped so much of my young spirit survive, and it still guides me.

SHARON TODAY

Sharon Abra Hanen kept her young adult self going on music, books, photography, optimistic efforts at drama productions, and friends that stretched her imagination. She's been a bicycle courier (once), a sculptor's model (a few times), and an arts educator (quite a bit). Now she is a library-loving writer of picture books, poems, and novels for younger readers in which chocolate, night, grappling hooks, jazz music, and popcorn feature with statistically improbable frequency. She also works as a creative coach and communication consultant for artists, writers, and deep-thinking businesses, and she practices meditation and reiki.

LANGUAGE OF DANCE

By JANET GOLDBLATT HOLMES

Dear Janet,

I'm sitting here in the early hours of the morning, thinking about you. I miss you. The you that lived before the rape. The you that knew innocence, trust, a sense of spontaneity, and lightheartedness.

When you and your family went on that ski holiday, you were only sixteen. When standing in line with your younger sister, waiting for the chair lift, you heard someone call out, "Single?"—a tall, blonde-haired, cute skier, wearing mirrored sunglasses. How could you resist? Please try not to beat yourself up because you quickly raised your ski pole and called out, "Single," leaving your sister to fend for herself. Although your actions nag at you, poking at the tender issue of sibling relationships, going off with a stranger seemed okay.

By end of day, he asked if you would go out with him for dinner. Remember the excitement you felt to have met someone and to be asked out on a date? What could possibly go wrong? You had your parent's permission—he came by your hotel to pick you up and walk to a local restaurant.

After dinner, he invited you to his house, which he shared with other people. You were out of your comfort zone, but what harm could come from going to meet his friends? He was so polite—it was all so ordinary.

You trusted him—you'd been on dates at home before. At the time, you were a virgin and had a fantasy of love based on Hollywood and Disney films. Sex was the farthest thing from your mind. You tried to stop him. Your repeated pleas of "No," "I'm a virgin," "I'm not ready to have sex," were to no avail. You froze. You had your hands over your pubic bone, thinking the pressure you felt was merely his body weight.

I am so sorry that you felt you didn't have the strength to push him off, and I understand the denial—that if nothing happened that night, then nothing did. That is what you needed to tell yourself.

Please do not judge yourself too harshly.

You'll find your way out of this through many forms. You've always loved to dance. Immersing yourself in the joy of movement. When dancing, you are free, spontaneous, have confidence, and your core strength emerges. In control of your body, mind, and spirit, you find a place of power, peace, and calm. Often you feel that dance is your haven. Your commitment to this will save you in many ways, although you won't recognize that until later.

When in a class or studio, you will find yourself at home in your body. The language of modern dance speaks to you: rise and fall, body weight propels you fluidly through swings, turns, and spirals. Whether to percussive rhythms of the drums or the lyrical melody of classical piano, your body responds with pure joy.

Your instructors are positive, encouraging, offering critique in a gentle manner: "Great!" "Beautiful lines, Janet." "Not so good, try again—use your breath to expand and fill the space." This is so different than the reprimands and criticisms heard at home.

Still, the body holds memory, and you will become aware of your limitations the more you study the art of dance and the language of movement. You'll face that there are more layers which need to unfold in order to find the light and freedom you felt before the age of sixteen. Until then, you stand with the dancer's upright posture. The invisible weight you are carrying is undetectable to everyone.

You are intrigued with the concept of how the body holds memory and with various healing modalities that help a person release the traumatic impact from the body on a cellular level. You are introduced to how sound can open pathways in the body. You find someone to help you deal with the trauma of the rape—you confide that in instances when you feel threatened or backed into a corner, internally, "I freeze just like I did when I was raped."

Your mentor is someone with whom you have trust and feel safe. She takes you step-by-step through the night of the rape and at the instant you feel panic and stop your breath, she gently encourages you to breathe, "in and out, in and out," until your body slows and panic subsides. Like in dance, you need to breathe in order to move.

Encouraged to speak about what this means, you realize that in close relationships, a heated argument can trigger a fear reaction.

Wanting the conversation to end, you cover your ears yelling: "Stop, Stop." If the disagreement continues, your voice unheard, you feel your body go rigid. This is a huge recognition. This is freezing. It is not the fluid movement of the dancer: the tall spine, open chest, using the whole torso, allowing arms and legs to move with more freedom within the shoulder girdle, hips, and pelvic bowl.

Be proud of your willingness to persevere and navigate your way through the painful terrain. You do so when you are ready and able to trust. The gentle guidance of healers, alternative therapies, and continuing to immerse yourself in dance, art, and writing will help you regain your strength and power.

There will be times, however, that memory is stirred, images haunt, and the past resurfaces. You will think the rape was your fault. Please recognize that saying no, even once, is enough to be heard. You were raised to be "perfect" and behave in a certain way, act like a "lady." How could you tell your parents or siblings? They wouldn't understand, let alone offer any emotional support—the pressure overwhelming, you repeatedly question your actions.

During these moments, be gentle and kind with yourself. Remember that healing takes time; it's like peeling back an onion, layer by layer. Your lightheartedness will return. Just like the freedom of traveling across the dance floor: You will fall, roll, rise.

As I continue to think about you, I want to tell you that in the future, you will heal and become the woman you aspired to be as a young girl. You will find your voice. You will understand that, although the violence that happened to you can never be erased, you can learn to live with the reality and know that although you *were* a victim of a violent crime, you have control over your body. You have leaped, turned, spiraled, jumped, and sweated your way to the future. You are no longer a victim.

You are a survivor.

With love,

Your adult self

————————

JANET UNFILTERED
LAYERS

Janet, you mention that, after the rape, you were in denial. Did you realize immediately that you had been sexually assaulted?
No, I had no idea that what happened was rape—I just knew that it was wrong. Seven or eight years after the rape, in my midtwenties, people were talking about "date rape," a new term. This is when I realized, from the various examples discussed, that this is what had happened to me. Still, not until I was in my forties did I truly realize what had happened, and thus was able to begin to heal.

How is recovery going?
Recovery is an interesting term, and *fully recovered*—is one ever fully recovered from a trauma? Healing is nonlinear, and therefore healing and recovery is an ongoing process. At times memory of the incident can be triggered, especially when coverage of sexual assault is in the news. Today, I am better able to recognize when or what triggers the memory of the rape and to mindfully bring myself to the present moment.

In this piece, you describe the safety of the dance studio as a very important part of your recovery and self-expression. What else helped you get through it?
There were so many layers to peel back—so much I had locked away inside my body on a cellular level. As a dancer, I was very aware of my body. In addition to training in contemporary dance, I also immersed myself in a variety of movement-based and alternative therapies. There was one treatment in my midfifties, almost forty years after the assault, that had a profound effect on me—I went to see a shaman healer. I spent so many years blaming myself for what happened, and the propensity to carry blame spilled over into other aspects of my life. During the session, I realized that if the healer could see inside of me and I was okay, then I was okay. Another is my work as an advocate and writing workshop coordinator with the Voices and Faces Project, which has allowed me to meet many other brave survivors who are also finding their voice. The work is

fulfilling, inspiring, empowering, and I feel like I've arrived home. I now have more trust and am safe enough to share more intimately with those I love.

In the spirit of advocacy, if you could give a piece of advice to a teen or kid in the same situation, what would it be?
Tell someone that you trust.

Know that you did nothing wrong.

You are loved, beautiful, precious, and good.

The road is long, painful, and lonely, but you are not alone.

I also realize, looking back, that in my situation, there was nothing else that I could have done. The truth was—there was no one in whom I could confide, which is a difficult and sad realization. I would also offer that being kind to ourselves is most important. We each have our way of healing, when we are ready. Trust your intuition. No matter how many people might offer suggestions or tell you what to do, or with whom to talk, until you are ready, you won't go. But please know, silence is the enemy of change, and the longer we bury the abuse, assault, or rape, the more we hurt ourselves. There is no need to carry the burden of shame.

JANET TODAY

Silent for forty years after surviving sexual violence and the abuse she lived through, Janet Goldblatt Holmes began to write about having survived rape. Her essays have been published in the United States, Canada, and Australia.

As a writer, artist, dancer, and educator, Janet believes that our voices are our most effective tools for creating change. She worked with children, adolescents, and young adults for many years, having developed an integrative arts approach, using dance, language, and expression to promote confidence and to discover one's voice.

Since 2010, Janet has worked closely with the Voices and Faces Project in the United States and Canada. She is currently the writing workshop outreach coordinator for the testimonial writing workshop "The Stories We Tell."

HUMMINGBIRD HEARTS
By CARRIE JONES

The weird thing about the heart is that fear and love both make it beat faster, but when it's fear that turns your heart into something that should be inside a tiny bird instead of a human, every single beat hurts.

Every single beat reminds you that you want to zip away, hide in some rosebush somewhere like Sleeping Beauty did, and surround yourself with thorns. It makes you wonder if Sleeping Beauty had a hummingbird heart, too. It makes you wonder if maybe you could follow her lead and sleep forever just so that you didn't have to deal with the pain of each hummingbird beat of your own heart.

Evolution of a Hummingbird

First, there was Uncle Al, one of my dad's friends. He would offer me lollipops and smash his crotch in my face. He smelled like engine grease, and his voice was louder than big trucks with missing mufflers.

We would visit him sometimes on Sundays, and my dad would hang out with all the guys in Uncle Al's basement. There was a pool table there. Everyone but my dad played pool. There was beer there. Everyone but my dad drank.

Sometimes Uncle Al wouldn't just smash his crotch in my face; sometimes he would whisper and grab my chest. "Uncle Al is the kiddie's pal, isn't that right, Carriekins?"

I told my mom that I didn't like Uncle Al.

She said, "Nobody does, honey."

But my dad did.

I was in first grade. I stopped liking bears because bears were big and hairy like Uncle Al was big and hairy. Bears growled like Uncle Al growled. Hummingbirds were so small next to bears, too small.

Then there was Uncle Joe, a stepuncle who traveled all the way across the country to visit us. The day he got to our house my stepdad died. Uncle Joe didn't seem too sad. The night after, he laid on top of me while I tried to sleep. He smooshed me beneath him and wiggled.

I was in fifth grade. I didn't know what was happening. I just knew I was trapped.

"We are both sad, baby." His breath was margaritas and cigarettes when he spoke.

All my ribs seemed to crack under him and I couldn't move. My nose and mouth were trapped beneath a sweaty T-shirt, making it seem impossible to breathe. *Sometimes cats strike hummingbirds out of the sky and they fall, stunned and motionless to the ground. The only thing that keeps moving is their hearts.*

"Why don't we make each other less sad," he suggested. I just cried, but I was so smothered beneath him that my tears couldn't run down my cheeks. They pooled there in my eyes.

And then I knew that it didn't matter if I could move or not because I was already dead. I stopped liking funny guys who wore suspenders because Uncle Joe was all the way from California and wore suspenders and made jokes. My mother gave him my stepfather's car. I hoped he would die when he drove back. He didn't.

"Evil never dies," my nana always said. Her yard was filled with hummingbird feeders. They dangled from tree limbs, from thin metal stands. When the hummingbirds died, we would bury them out by the rhubarb. They must not have been evil.

There was Mike right before college. I felt badly for him because he had a hang-dog face and beagle-dog eyes, and he never ever seemed happy. He hated his dad. I went to a party, and he got drunk and threw me over his shoulder and marched upstairs, pretending to everyone that it was a joke as I screamed. They believed him. It is surprisingly easy for people to not believe hummingbird screams.

"Shut up," he said.

"Nobody can hear you," he said.

"You are a nothing girl," he said.

And it hurt so much because I tried to move and fight. It hurt so much because I didn't know how to move or fight. I had been dead so long.

That is why hummingbirds have to be quick.

That is why hummingbirds have to learn to bob and weave with every beat of their frantic hearts.

That is why hummingbird hearts remind them "Danger, danger" in every fast pulse.

That is why hummingbird hearts remind them, "You are alive. Listen. Listen! Move."

Hummingbirds Have a History of Being Killed for Their Feathers

If you tell your truth, people will call you things like "victim," "whore," "survivor." You don't need to listen to those people. Hummingbirds have the ability to fly away from labels.

If you tell your truth, your heart might feel too big for a hummingbird's body—so big that it's about to crack open. If it does, you can stitch it back up again.

If you don't tell your truth, your heart might start to shrivel into itself, drying up. If it does, you can reinflate it. I promise.

Hummingbirds Remember Every Flower They've Met

People will ask you things:

Didn't you say no?

Did it hurt?

Do you want to kill him?

Do you know that one out of four women in this country gets raped?

Do you want to see a counselor?

Do you want to see a doctor?

Do you want to file a report?

How do you go on?

People will tell you things:

Don't make it a big deal.

Make it a big deal.

Don't let it define you.

It defines you.

Tell me everything.

Tell me nothing.

Migration

Hummingbirds move. We migrate every year. A small hummingbird can flap her wings fifty-five times in one second. We can fly twenty-five miles per hour. When we dive, we go sixty. That's how it is with diving. Gravity can pull even the lightest of us down faster. And our hearts? They secretly can stand the pressure. That's why we survive.

Our hearts beat 1,260 times in a minute. But when we are still—and we can be still—they lower to just fifty beats.

And the other thing? We are not the same, we hummingbirds; our paths are different, our movements, our stories, but there are more than 325 species of hummingbirds in the world. Some of us are broad-tailed. Some of us are ruby-throated or white-eared. Some of us are black-chinned or violet-crowned or just magnificent.

We may not be able to walk or hop, but we can scoot sideways. We can soar and flutter and hover the way nobody else can. We are small, but we can survive.

CARRIE UNFILTERED
GOOD FRIENDS AND BAD POETRY

Carrie, you describe multiple painful experiences in this piece. Did you ever tell anyone about them? Who was the first person you told, and was this the same as the first person who heard you?
The first person I told about the Uncle Joe incident was my mom. She told me that people grieve in strange ways and that my stepuncle was heading back to California soon. She refused to talk about it. I think all I got out was, "Uncle Joe did something." The first person who heard me was my seventh-grade social studies teacher, Mr. Faichney.

I'm thankful for the Mr. Faichney's of the world. Having someone hear you often seems to be the first step to validation and recovery. At this point, do you feel that you are fully recovered?
I am so good at repressing things. I mean, I began to repress it the first day after it happened—the Uncle Joe incident again. I never saw him again, but I heard that something had happened with him and two of my stepcousins in Louisiana, girls I had never met. I think I am fully recovered, but then I will catch myself Googling his name. And then I'll be all, "Where did that come from?"

Did you report any of the crimes?
I didn't know that I could when I was little. With the rape, I didn't. I didn't have the strength.

Thinking back, are there any resources, information, or awareness that might have helped you have the strength to go to the police?
I would like to say yes, but that wouldn't be the whole truth. I honestly don't know. I'm not the person I was then.

The thought of talking to members of that all-male police department was not something I had any desire to do when it happened. It was hard for me to trust strange men after men I knew had hurt me. I think that making sure that there are female officers and making sure the community knows about their presence would help female survivors of sexual assault. I think that if each police department could manage to have at least one female officer trained for these cases, it would help. There are far too few female officers where I live even now.

What coping mechanisms did you use during recovery, and how did they help?
When I was in college, my boyfriend and I created a project in which we reenacted a date rape on campus. Maine Supreme Court justices and district attorneys volunteered their time. My mom transposed the script. I played the woman who was raped. We basically improvised an entire trial. Tons of people were there. The news media came, and my poor nana saw a clip on the news and had no idea that it wasn't a real trial. Anyway, that was a good meld of art and truth that I could participate in and orchestrate. It was powerful and it was healing. I also wrote *a massive ton* of really bad poems. Poems that started with lines like, "You are vampire / vamping with your struts and smiles / you flaunt your sex and fly / across the Crayola-colored sky / of my backyard." It was really bad stuff. This is why I'm not a poet.

One thing you raise throughout this piece is how others try to define you. Sometimes very negatively. After the assaults, did you run into this victim-blaming attitude?

The thing is, I didn't with any of my close friends. Apparently, I chose my friends so wisely. I was really lucky that way.

When I was finally brave enough to tell my friends about the things that had happened to me, they wanted details. They asked questions. They wanted to understand why it had happened, which sometimes felt overwhelming to me because I didn't understand why it had happened, either. It was a story that was difficult to tell because I didn't want to relive it in the telling.

The few friends I told were the opposite of victim blaming. Some of them wanted vengeance. Some of them wanted to be heroes. They all desperately wanted to make things better somehow, to make things right. I was so lucky to have such beautiful and amazing friends.

CARRIE TODAY

New York Times and internationally bestselling author Carrie Jones writes novels for children and young adults, including the *Need, Flying,* and *Time Stoppers* series. Some of these books have won awards. A lot of them involve girls being heroes and friends being awesome. She also is the coeditor of *Dear Bully,* an anthology of authors sharing their stories about bullying. She lives in Maine where she is an on-call firefighter, human rights advocate, and the regional public image chair for Rotary International. She has a lot of rescue dogs and one potato-loving cat.

PEARLS OF WISDOM
By LAURA H. KELLY

At my all-girls high school, my favorite teacher taught chemistry, of all things! Yep, I was one of those geeky science kids. Honestly, though, I think Mrs. K would have been my favorite even if she taught history, the subject I liked least. She was around sixty years old, had short white hair, a no-nonsense attitude, and eyes in the back of her head. Nothing ever slipped by her, and we couldn't get away with any shortcuts, which probably made our chemistry lab a safer place, if you think about it. She loved us, believed in us, and had high standards for our work, which meant when she praised you it was worth something.

What I loved about Mrs. K though was that she often started her classes with a story. Sometimes it would be related to a science topic, but usually it was a personal story about life—what it meant to be a woman in the world. And these ended with a piece of advice, which she called a "Pearl of Wisdom." I can't remember any of her pearls now; the details weren't important, anyway. What I can remember clearly was the sight of her at the front of the classroom, leaning on the lab counter by the sink, wearing her white lab coat, telling a humorous story, smirking, and giving guidance to students she felt were worth instructing on more than just science lessons. I remember the feeling of mutual respect.

So, in the spirit of Mrs. K, I'd like to give you some of my Pearls of Wisdom on the topic of incest.

First pearl of wisdom: Believe in yourself, you are important, and your life matters. Allow yourself to dream of a future.
When I was in elementary school, I would soothe myself at bedtime with my own made-up fairy tale. I imagined that while I was sleeping soundly in a four-poster bed, hundreds of princes would come from miles around, line up to get a little peek at me (and the line would snake out of the house and down the block), and then they would leave beautiful and fancy gifts under my bed—jewelry

and gowns and delicious chocolate candies and books. I had a favorite Cinderella book with delicate feathery illustrations, and I wanted a ball gown in rose pink and gold, like she wore. I wanted to be just like that Cinderella with long wavy hair, a jeweled tiara, and candied fruit to eat. Then in my fairy tale, I would wake up to find out I was really a princess and everyone loved me, and I could run away with the most handsome prince. I would make the ones with the best gifts line up so I could choose which man to marry. I desperately needed to get away, though if anyone asked me what from, I couldn't have said. I thought of myself as being rescued and protected, but I needed the prince to prove his worth, too, and to cherish me.

As a child, I never shared my bedtime tale with anyone, just like I didn't talk about the games that my father made me play naked with him.

By the time I was thirteen—when, finally, I had to admit to myself that my bedtime story was childish and silly—I would imagine other ways of escape. I would fantasize riding off on a powerful red motorcycle as far as its wheels would take me. I had never been *on* a motorcycle, mind you, and knew nothing of makes or models, but I imagined it would be a powerful fast bicycle that I could ride without tiring for a thousand miles, with my long hair streaming behind me in the whistling wind—and it had to be candy apple red. Or I would try to visualize what college would be like, hoping to become a famous scientist and discover the cure for cancer. I'd be bent over my chemistry lab work, deep in thought, smelling of noxious chemicals, but with all my labmates impressed with my important discoveries and formulas. My dreams had shifted from hoping for someone to rescue me to planning to set myself free.

My father molested me hundreds of times between the ages of four and fifteen. I can't remember each individual time any more than anyone can count the fish in the sea. It started out playful, taking baths together and games at bedtime. Later it got more serious. I would call what happened when I was fifteen "rape," and I was afraid of getting pregnant. Unwanted sexual contact happened almost weekly for eleven years, and I never said a word. I couldn't! I was afraid that my whole world would fall apart if I did. The molesting stopped when I was fifteen only because of an accident, and I had to be in the hospital for several months. The accident shocked my father into good behavior and broke the habit. I wish I could say someone rescued me, or that I myself managed to get it to stop, but it was just dumb luck.

Both my strategies for soothing myself—the princess story and the dream of being a famous scientist—sound like I was really full of myself, and perhaps I did think too highly of my own merits and beauty. However, they have one thing in common—they kept reminding me I was worth something. Possibly I had a few places (like school) and people (like Mrs. K and my grandmother) who gave me praise, or perhaps it was my optimistic personality; doesn't matter. Either way, I had just enough self-esteem to see me through rough times.

I never became famous, in science or any other field, and I never married a prince (2 marriages, 0 princes!). But I survived, and I am happy with who I am. And you will, too, and your life can be what you make it. Believe in yourself.

Second pearl of wisdom: Forgive yourself. Sometimes there are no good choices.
What my father did was terrible, but being with my mother was not any better. She was the kind of mother who deliberately would buy cookies that none of us kids liked because they lasted longer. Of course, they were ones she liked, and in the evening she would have two or three, while we watched, and the horrid package lasted weeks. "You wanted cookies, I bought cookies. You can eat them or not."

Often, after my parents had a nasty, loud argument, she would load me and my siblings in the Chevrolet wagon and take us house hunting because she was going to leave him *once and for all!* We would fight among ourselves for the spot in the back seat behind her, since it was the only seat where she could not bend her arm back enough to hit us. The shotgun seat was the worst spot! She was "driving angry," and I feared she would crash the car into a tree. I feared for my life.

Almost every adult in your life, and most survivors of molestation, will tell you that if you are being abused, you need to report it and get it to stop. But this is extremely hard to do. It takes courage. The risk is very real that your life as you know it will change, and you can't anticipate or control how. For me, the fear was having to live with just my mom and her anger. Plus, I was afraid that if Dad left, it might hurt my chances of going to college. In the end I never did report him. Perhaps it was making a choice passively, but it seemed the right choice for me at the time.

The one regret I have in not reporting my father: I failed to protect my sister, who was five years younger than me—and for all I know, other little girls he came in contact with later—from the same fate. When I was around eight or nine, my father and I struck a deal that if I cooperated and kept silent, then he would leave her alone. He broke that promise, but I didn't know this until many, many years later. I've learned that pedophiles only make rules that suit themselves, and they only hold promises when it serves them. We believe them because we're kids, and it's a hard spot to be in, where you don't have a parent to turn to or trust. My sister and I are friends still, and I've had to forgive myself for not being a better big sister. Because I was just a kid then, too.

You are still young and have a lot of life ahead of you. To get on with your wonderful full life, you have to forgive yourself for the past. You don't have to forgive whoever has molested you! You have to forgive yourself for the choices you made, and the decisions you did or didn't make, and move on.

Third pearl of wisdom: Most people will believe you are telling the truth, and there are many good people in the world.
Most people are good—really, they are. You can trust them to do their best to help you. They won't be perfect, but they will do what they can. You will feel immense relief when you finally can talk, and you will feel less lonely.

I wasn't being molested anymore, but in the three years between my hospital stay and when I gathered the courage to tell people, I began to think I had imagined it all as some sick nightmare, or maybe I was going crazy. I was totally surprised, when I finally started telling people, that everyone believed me, supported me, and loved me, anyway—my college boyfriend, girlfriends, a counselor. That was the beginning of my healing. Now I can tell anyone and everyone what happened if I want to, and it's okay. I even forget who I've told and who I haven't. The hardest folks to tell, though, are the first few. The number-one hardest person to tell was my mother, and I never did, though she found out accidentally years later, reading my private mail without permission, and she was still angry. You have to get over the hurdle of trusting someone else, and take a leap of faith. But overall, people are good and on your side.

Last pearl of wisdom: The experiences you have been through are not your fault. You are not being punished, and you are not bad or dirty.
You got handed a bad deck of cards when you were born. You got plopped down into a family with a pedophile and perhaps a self-centered blind mother as well, and they are great at making you feel like everything is your fault.

It isn't.

As a result, though, you have some strengths. I bet you are more independent than other kids your age and can handle more frustration and pain. These will serve you well. The deck is stacked with a lot of pain to overcome, too. But you are tough and can do it.

Think about what you want from life and hang on to that dream. It is okay to dream and plan for your future. What is that phrase? "Shoot for the moon, and you'll fall in the stars. Shoot for the barnyard door, and you'll fall in the shit." Dream big. What happened to you is real, but not all people are bad, and many will be on your side. Soon you will be free. You deserve a good life, and if you let yourself imagine that good life and work toward it, you'll get there.

The Four Pearls
In my high school yearbook, Mrs. K wrote, "I expect to be hearing great things from you in the future. The best of everything. Affectionately, Mrs. K." I imagine she was thinking of those "great things" in the field of science, but she didn't really say so. I almost would hate to tell her that I never became a scientist; I'd hate to disappoint her. But I think she would approve of my pearls of wisdom today, and if I could, I'd ask her, "Did I do okay, Mrs. K?"

LAURA UNFILTERED
LIFE IS GOOD

Laura, when abuse starts at such a young age, it seems very hard to differentiate between what is normal and what is not. At what point did you realize that you were being abused?
I have no clear memory of when I knew the games my father and I played were not okay. This is a real problem with incest or familial molestation—it often starts before the child has the words for what is happening or a sense of what is right and wrong. I was instructed to keep a secret when very young, and certainly by age eight, I knew it was wrong because I started hiding from him when he and I were the only ones in the house. But I still couldn't have called it assault. I just knew I didn't like it. It started to feel like assault (like an attack) when I began to protest and fight back, which I think was when I was around twelve, because that's when he got aggressive. Now, I'd call what happened at age four (taking baths together) assault, but it took years for me to see it that way. Assault isn't just violence. It's any age-inappropriate sexual contact, even between peers, when one is using their power to take advantage of another to do things against their will.

Who was the first person you told, and did that person hear you?
Being molested made me familiar with male bodies and sex, but not in a good way. I avoided boys my age. My life was sheltered. I attended an all girls' high school, so not seeing boys wasn't hard. But when I got to college, living on campus, I wanted to have sex and love like everyone else. I was curious, and aroused, and fell in love numerous times. For a while, I was going out with a boy who had a secretive side. He was exotic, from Peru, a smooth dancer, sexy, and oh so smart. One night while we were lying in his narrow dorm room bed together, I asked him if he had any secrets. I proposed a swap: If he told me his secret, I'd tell him mine. Turned out he was bisexual, but he hadn't yet been out with a man. His coming out to me was the beginning of a new adventure for him. And for the first time, I told someone I had been molested by my father. Yes, my friend heard me, was angry on my behalf, but understanding and comforting, too. He accepted me as I was, and I accepted him.

You talk about getting on with your wonderful life. I like that wording. So life is good?

Hell, yeah! Life is good. The fact I have this incest history does not define who I am and what I do. But I still have PTSD moments, probably always will. Think of it this way—PTSD is like a muscle memory, a physical thing you can't control. Let me give you an example: Suppose you see a house on fire. Your body is going to react—to be afraid for your safety, worried if someone is inside, excited because of the commotion, and your adrenaline will be pumping. You might then back up to a safe distance. Some people will do the opposite without a moment's hesitation and run into the burning house to rescue a child. Some will call 911 immediately; others will freeze and not be able to move. All of these are physical reactions to trauma, and normal. PTSD, though, is when some later event triggers those body memories of the more traumatic event. The trigger might be similar but not dangerous—like seeing a campfire. Or it might be something that seems totally innocuous— like seeing a house that has the same shape as the one that burned down. Or the trigger could be hearing a story exactly like the one you experienced—of someone inside a burning house. Before your brain registers what is going on, your body has reacted. So, it's very hard to totally get rid of PTSD, but it is possible to recognize what is happening and talk your way out of it. "Okay, I'm getting anxious here, why? I see, it's a fire again, yes, only a campfire—contained in a firepit. We're doing this safely, I'm safe, I'm not alone. I can roast marshmallows now."

There is a lot of public awareness of PTSD these days, and books and websites are sometimes labeled with "trigger warnings." Have you ever had PTSD from reading something, in a book or online, and do you find these trigger warnings helpful?

When I was a teenager, lots of things would trigger me because I didn't yet have a place to talk about what was going on at home. The more I talked about my whole experience, the easier my PTSD got. I don't get triggered by reading that much, but I know others who do. For me, the triggers are more situational, where I see people or even animals that are in danger, or I myself feel trapped and have no control. An example might be if I got a flat tire in my car at night, and I don't want to get out of my car because that feels unsafe, and yet I feel trapped inside the car. Then, waiting a long time for assistance, and having to rely on help from strangers, that would trigger me. It takes me back to my dad holding me down, and I had no escape. Everyone is different, though. So, I think trigger warnings on books are useful because they reduce the element of surprise, especially if they give more detail—"trigger warning, graphic sexual violence."

Is there anything you want to say that I haven't covered?
Oh, I really want to say this to all sexual abuse survivors: You probably aren't thinking about this now, but you might one day. Someday I hope you marry and have children. It's a wonderful feeling to share your life with someone, and little kids are delightful. Choose your partner carefully, and don't rush. I had trouble trusting men, and I had no idea what I wanted in a husband. I married too young, and my marriage didn't last. But we had some wonderful children together, who are healthy and happy. Recognize that being molested might influence how you think and what you do, double check your actions, and take your time. I was anxious when my son went camping with Scouts, and I'd wonder, "Can I trust those Scout leaders?" So, I got to know them, and I talked to my son about "good touch, bad touch" without scaring him. My fear of what could happen was strong, and I had to do reality checks all the time. It doesn't hurt to be watchful, and most people are trustworthy. For those of you who worry (I did!) that you won't know how to be a good parent with no role models—you can do it! Trust your instincts. Allow yourself to live a normal life and be happy.

LAURA H. TODAY

Laura H. Kelly grew up in Philadelphia, was educated at MIT, then received a master's in clinical psychology, but she decided that being a stay-at-home mom was her calling. She enjoys reading all types of fiction, good food, and dancing. There are always flowers blooming in her San Diego garden, and friends over for happy hour in the patio. The house is decorated with bright-colored windsocks, friendly whirly-gigs, and tinkling chimes. What does Laura drive now? Sadly, not a motorcycle, but a practical little Volvo wagon—color? *Red,* of course! She dreams that one day she'll go on a "round the world" cruise. She's currently working on a memoir.

I KNOW
By ASTER LEE

Dear Little One,
Everything is going to be okay. You're going to make it out of here.
Can you believe it? These years of living in fear, these years of being
paranoid at night, in a place you call "home." In the shower, in your
room—you survive—in fact, you do more than just survive; you
conquer it!

I know you are frightened. I know you feel so alone. You do
all that you can to survive and to live every single day. It is difficult,
but you don't know anything different—this is your "normal," even
though there is nothing normal about it. It just *is,* for you. You do
what you have to do and no child in the world should have to think
about surviving in her own home.

I want you to know that you are more than what is happening to
you. You are the kid who has the best Lisa Frank sticker collection.
You are the kid who loves to sing along to your favorite song on the
radio. Mostly, you are the kid who enjoys making those around you
laugh. You love being a big sister. How you adore your little sister.
You share a room, and sure, she gets on your nerves, but you two
are inseparable. The two of you stay up, just talking for hours about
everything—like her new crush at school, your favorite band (you
both love Hanson), or what is happening over the weekend.

I know you never want the conversations to end. The long
silence that greets you after she falls asleep is like that unwanted
guest who never wants to leave. You stare out of the small window as
you lie under the blue plaid comforter, carefully tugging it over you
as you snuggle into it for extra cover, trying not to make too much
noise, eyes wide open and searching for the shiniest of stars to make
a wish on.

I wish he would just hit me. Please just let him hit me next time.
You repeat this over and over and over until you fall into deep
sleep. I understand you, my love. All you ever want is someone who
loves and protects you. He is supposed to be your protector.

I know the nights are never easy. They are dark. And the darkness finds a way to cling to you, even in the day.

I can tell you that the darkness never truly goes away, but it does fade and come less often. I know the happy face you wear becomes routine; I know how much you want to take off that mask, especially during Thanksgiving, which is your favorite holiday, but you are afraid of what could happen if it comes off. I know that sometimes it is easy to pretend happiness when you are surrounded by distractions like your little brother, cousins, your favorite aunt, and the latest Nintendo games. I know that pretend life can sometimes be sweet and comforting, just to feel the semblance of what normal could be like, even for a moment.

But there will be a time when the pretending is no longer the majority of the time. The road ahead will continue to teach you about yourself, and it will be an incredible experience. You will come to meet the most kind and supportive of people—those who have earned the love and place in your life.

The relationship with your little sister will be one of your most treasured things in life. I can't wait for you to have that again. And there will be other things, too. You will be eager to learn about the world you live in. You will be an individual who enjoys fruitful and provoking conversations over dinner with your closest friends and significant other; an individual who discovers yourself through helping others, and who finds joy in the small moments, like a fresh morning cup of coffee.

Please know that none of this is your fault. Please know that there will be bright spots in the future. There will be cups of dark roast coffee. There will be strong relationships and exciting conversations. And there will be wishes that do come true. Beautiful things happen because of you. I promise to do my best to honor you.

With all my heart,
Aster

ASTER UNFILTERED
SISTER SOLACE

Aster, you bring us through a painful childhood that has pockets of sweet and comforting moments. Your letter to young Aster is lined with encouragement that there are better times ahead. Was there a breakthrough moment where you knew you would be okay?
I think I had a few of these "breakthrough" moments because I think it depends on what else is happening in my life and what developmental stage I am in. Going through the abuse and even years afterward, there were a lot of suppressed thoughts and feelings because it was so normal to me, as frightening as it sounds stating that right now. It wasn't until I was in college that the memories from the abuse began to surface. My very first breakthrough moment when I knew I would be okay was when I told my sister. It was and still is the scariest and most difficult thing I have ever done in my life thus far. I remember the anticipation of it and the moments leading up to when I told her. I physiologically felt ill because I was so scared for so many reasons. I was shaking, my stomach was churning, and I felt like I was going to vomit. I consider this a breakthrough because she is the one person that I cared about the most, and I wanted her to know who I am, who I really am. When the words came out of my mouth, it felt like I had just been rescued out of a dark, dark, lonely cave and was finally seen.

What was her response like?
After those words exited my mouth in between cries, my sister immediately sobbed and gave me a hug. We were holding hands the entire time as I prepared myself to tell her, and we didn't let go. She looked at me and said, "I'm so sorry," and continued to cry. It felt as though she was crying for me and the young Aster. That was my breakthrough moment.

Your sister sounds like a great ally. Can you give any advice to people who want to be allies?
If there is one thing I could tell people outside of this experience, it is that it is okay to ask how we are doing, especially if the survivor

has opened up herself or himself to you one way or another, and that it won't make things harder just by bringing it up. It just shows that you care, and it is something that you're aware and cognizant of. It's important to educate yourself about different kinds of traumas and how they affect the individuals over time. There are traumas that are publicized and less controversial, and there are others that cannot be seen or talked about. Those who want to be allies with survivors, I thank you in advance because we need people like you to speak for us, for many of us still feel silenced, unheard, and unsupported. It is important to remove the stigma of sexual assault and sexual abuse, and survivors can't do it on our own, so thank you.

You and your sister loved Hanson. In a way, their music got you through some hard times. Did other music or artists help, too?
When I turned fifteen years old, my parents bought me my first boombox—it was gigantic—and it was then when I had a choice of music I could listen to. This was the midnineties when people were still buying CDs! My uncle had the "Best of Michael Jackson" CD collection, and he gave it to me for my birthday. I began to listen to it and fell in love with "Heal the World." I would impatiently wait to get on the school bus to come home so I could just go into my room, shut the door, put on my large headphones, and turn up "Heal the World" by Michael Jackson. I don't think I realized it then but that song helped me get through high school because it provided me a few minutes of comfort, predictability, and hope. I remember being fifteen years old and thinking about how wonderful it would be if we had a world like what Michael Jackson sang about, that there was something much greater than my fifteen-year-old self sitting in my room, and I wanted to be part of that some day.

You've already written such powerful encouragement to a younger you. Now, if you could give a piece of advice to a teen or kid in the same situation, what would it be?
You are probably the strongest person you know, and I am not exaggerating. In fact, I guarantee that you are *the* strongest person you have ever come across. Life will continue to feel tough, and it'll feel like something in the universe is working against you, making it difficult to get through the days, weeks, months, and years, but

you will come out of it. You must allow yourself the time to heal and recover and find just one or two people who you love, trust, respect, and value, and tell them about your past because they will listen to you without judgment, and only love. Sometimes it feels easier to be on your own, to be independent and detached from people in your life, but life is not about that—we are meant for connections. Although you can and should learn to connect with yourself, sometimes we need those additional hands and hearts to be there for us, too. Sometimes, you will find it hard to be lovable, that you're not worth it, but know that you *are* lovable and worth it. You are the strongest person you will ever know. Lastly, if you feel thoughts of suicide, and those negative thoughts of wanting to hurt yourself seem to occupy your headspace, please reach out to someone you trust. Please do not feel alone because you are not. The reason I wanted to share my story is because I believe that people should not suffer alone and should not feel like they are the only ones. You have a tribe out there, and even though you feel like you are the only one fighting, we are out there with you with our invisible swords.

ASTER TODAY

Aster Lee is a native of California but sees herself as a citizen of the world. While she loves her home state, every once in a while she loves to travel to a new place to discover and learn about different cultures, meet new people, and try unique foods. Aster is the eldest of three children; therefore, she considers herself to be a lot wiser than her younger sister and brother, whom she loves dearly but doesn't always agree with. Aster believes compassion grows from truly believing that every single person has their own unique story, fears, joys, and dreams. Aster's spirit animal is an elephant because she once heard that elephants never forget, and they remember if their friends experience hardships and sadness. Aster's favorite food in the whole wide world is her mom's homemade spaghetti. She can have that every single day of her life and never become tired of it. Aster currently lives in Southern California with her significant other.

SLEEP WELL

By ALLISON MALONEY

To the boy who sodomized me in the early 2000s,

The last time we spoke came by way of digital blurb: A request to *chill* during your visit to the Midwest, where I'd moved for college to distance myself from you and the smothering Southern box in which we were raised. It's gone unanswered for six years, but expect no apology within this reply, as this is a *fuck you* letter.

The things I remember most about you come as flashes unhooked from a detailed narrative, invoked involuntarily or played in synaptic loop-de-loops of memory my brain insists on showing before sleep. I cannot remember meeting you for the first time. I am unable to recall how our relationship came to end. All I can see, when I let you back into my brain, is the makings of your manipulation of my body and the phases of my own recovery as it's come to slowly pass. I did not realize you raped me until I was an adult, a decade after it happened. But then, in front of the mirror and the sink in the maybe-orange bathroom of my next-door neighbor's home, I was only a child.

I know that when we met I was barely a teenager, and I was entirely in love with you. You recognized my idolatry and preyed on me through AOL Instant Messenger, your attention causing dozens of arguments between my siblings and me when I'd childishly beg for more screen time. We both grew up in the heat of fields and shade of pine trees, children of the outdoors plagued by familial troubles and taken by words that filled books, turning pages to pass the time. I was happiest with my sister Sarah or alone. A moody temperament did not define me then as it does now.

The first flash, bright and hot in my skull, takes me to some high school event before the start of freshman year. I'm protected by a sleeping bag next to you and pretending to see the stars on a football field under stadium lights that stayed on throughout the night. There was stuffy warmth in the air, as there always was. An older girl, someone I felt I was in competition with because we shared a name, liked you as well, but you were laying next to *me*. I felt victorious.

Later that summer, my best friend was in the passenger's seat of that girl's car when she skidded through a pool of water that flipped her tires to the sky, pushing both of their trapped bodies over a median and into oncoming traffic. They died a year after my parents divorced, a month after the self-inflicted death of the man who was to be my principal, and weeks after separate accidents that nearly killed two other young people in our town. Middle school's sense of small ended with impactful, sudden violence. The feelings in and around me were reasonably raw, and I learned that to trust, to believe in stability, was to risk having all of the goodness snatched away.

But I trusted you.

Another flash: I'm waiting alone in my driveway on a Saturday after a promise that you would come see me was scrawled in a notebook we passed back and forth across desks. I couldn't yet drive, and I guess I feel stupid now, looking back at the size of my want and the longing I felt staring out into the gravel path I craved to hear your footsteps on. Flash to next Monday in a foreign-language class, you told me *I couldn't* across the pages of a notebook—one that sits stored but not forgotten now in the basement of my adulthood, pieces of paper it would sting to revisit.

There was another girl you loved, but she sometimes couldn't be bothered, so instead you played with me. I took up your game and wrapped myself in it because you looked like Jim Morrison, made me laugh like my dad, and I didn't know any better. I felt lucky that you showed up to the house where you raped me because it meant I'd called and you'd answered—proof I could make things *happen*, a powerful feeling—and it came as evidence that you liked me.

The memory of rape comes in two parts. In the first, we're on stools in the basement of my neighbor's home under a *Face/Off* poster featuring the wall-sized faces of Nicholas Cage and John Travolta. I am able to make out your sharp profile and the can in your hand from a glow produced by a string of Christmas lights. The second spark comes and we're up one floor, and I see the burnt-orange bathroom tile—or maybe it was the color of the wall—and hear you telling me what you're going to do. I see my own face reflecting back for one fraction of one-half of one second. I don't know what happened before or after, how we got there, if you left, what school felt like, or the next day, or the next day, or the next day. I know you fucked my ass even though I didn't want you to.

Both parts combined, the most paralyzing flash is the shortest I have. For this I am grateful.

I see another room in a flash where you showed me how to smoke weed from a Bic pen. When your attention was given, there was an unspoken demand for me to listen and learn—an early experience with *mansplaining*—and an implication that I was lucky to be in your air. Some flashes show no sign of your face, like the one two years ago in a city on the opposite coast, where I was lonely and old enough to drink, so I share with a beloved mutual childhood friend what you did to me so long ago, and he stands up for you. That other boy was a giant to me then, when I was still living with the youthful, misguided notion that one must keep in touch with every person they've ever known. I'm more disappointed in him than I ever have been in you.

The last spark is set on the edge of a soccer field that has cleared, and I'm about to board a white bus after recording the game's score—a duty I was prescribed after some insistence on my part in an effort to be close to boys, maybe you. Your sex has served as impetus to a wide range of engagements that never served me, to advantages taken without my full understanding. I never wanted to travel down the bumpy road of badness that got me named School Slut, but there I am as you untie your cleats. The sun is shining and my hair is darker than it was when we first met because I am desperate for change I can control. I say something about another girl's promiscuity, and you tell me that *the pot has called the kettle black*. This is the memory that plays the longest, the most intense one that I truly can't unsee.

As I said at the beginning of this letter to you: I did not recognize the implications of your actions until I was in my twenties after I was raped in a way that left little room for any amount of *well, maybe*. I started piecing together the connection between my negative relationship to sex, tracing the line further and further back to the start of my experiences and ultimately, back to that bathroom with you. I see my face in that mirror again, but I treat it with tenderness and see you as an asshole. I have lived through other assaults, suffered at the hands of other men. I have been thrown through years of flashes that compound to continuously suck the life out of me, but I've learned that I was given an original value at a formative age by a boy I loved who mortified me before and after he used my body.

That boy is you.

Sleep well,

Allison Maloney

ALLISON UNFILTERED
FEMINIST REFUGE

Alli, who was the first person you told? Did that person hear you?
I can't remember telling anyone after it happened. From what I remember, I assumed that sex worked in the way it was presented to me here: Man does what he wants, I pretend to like it. I told my longtime friend Erin, who knew us both, when I was in my twenties. She heard me. Shortly after, I told the mutual male friend mentioned in the piece, who did not hear me.

Did you report the crime?
I did not. I knew little about rape outside of the narrative that it comes by way of attack by a stranger, therefore I could not adequately define my experience or my pain.

Where is your abuser now?
Somewhere in North Carolina working as a scientist. Here's hoping his little research boat sinks.

What was a resource you wish you had known about?
When I dream of hypotheticals wherein this rape did not happen, no resource that would serve me comes to mind. I wish *he* had access to resources to address his issues.

What could friends, peers, or parents have done in the aftermath of the assault that could have made life easier?
I did not tell anyone about the assault afterward. I wish other parents had been less judgmental of my promiscuity afterward, however, as I was obviously processing trauma on numerous fronts.

Who helped you the most, and what made their help so effective?
Writing by women on rape, feminism, and womanhood. It's effective because my experience is not singular. Understanding the culture at large around the world—the patriarchal structures that make rape so common—helps me feel less alone, though "rape/assault victim" is a depressing team to be on.

Any favorite titles you'd like to share?
All About Love by Bell Hooks was helpful.

ALLISON TODAY

Alli Maloney is a writer. She currently works as the news and politics editor at *Teen Vogue*. You can find her on twitter @allimaloney.

THINGS I HAVEN'T SAID
By MELISSA MARR

Dear —

    I used to want to hurt you, to break you, to give you the sort of nightmares I still have so many years later. I think it's normal, wanting that. Georgia, my first therapist, said it was. I believed her.

    That was my first response—a fantasy that I was the stronger one. I imagined that, despite weighing only a blink over a hundred pounds at the time, I would be able to push you away so forcefully that not only would I be safe but that *you* would be hurt. I imagined getting away, running to my father's gun cabinet, and being fast enough to get a gun. I timed myself . . . just in case you came back. I wanted to punish you. You took what wasn't yours. You broke something I don't know how to fix. You *hurt* me.

    I'm glad I was a virgin at the time. When I doubted my memory, I could look at that detail. Even if I *could* explain away your violence, even if I *could* explain that you must've misunderstood, even if somehow maybe I said yes accidentally, even if that was *all* true (and it's not), I wouldn't have given you my virginity.

    Afterward, when I heard about how you cared about me, when I heard that you wished I would talk to you, when I heard that you were *hurt* I remembered that fact like it was a shield from the lies. We had never dated. We had no relationship beyond strangers passing at concerts or parties. No matter how much I tried to rationalize it so a Bad Thing hadn't happened to me, there was no way to explain the one indisputable fact: I wouldn't have given you my virginity.

    Years later, I might've fucked a stranger. I did sometimes—to prove I could say no, to prove I could have sex without panicking, to feel close to someone without letting them into my life. I did a lot of stupid things in the years that followed. But that wasn't who I was when you showed up without invitation or warning that day. Then, I was barely a teenager, not even old enough to drive. I wouldn't have given you my body. I wouldn't have given my first time away to someone I'd never dated, never kissed, never known. I *didn't* give myself. You took it. You ignored my words and my struggles. You ignored my tears. You ignored my bleeding.

A part of me wishes I could tell you how much you owe me. Not for what you took, but for what I *didn't* take. You might not ever realize it, but you owe me your life. I sat outside your house a few years later. The man beside me that day was an ex-con who was . . . an awful human being. He had a shotgun in his hands and a knife in his lap. He wanted to kill you. I was drunk, and I'd told him about you. Killing you was going to be his gift to me, to show that he was committed to me. We drove to your house. I saw you. He did, too. I wanted to be the monster. I wanted to let you bleed on your floor. And he wanted to do it. He liked killing things.

I said no.

He listened . . . and you're alive because of it. I wish I could tell you that. I wish I could let you know that I *chose* to let you live. But I didn't actually do it for you. I wanted to let go of the way I felt inside. Choosing to let you live was the first major step in getting well. That doesn't mean it was easy or without setbacks. I still think of you more than I want, but the hatred isn't festering like it was then. Now, it's manageable. The hate still comes like an unexpected storm sometimes, but it passes.

And I deal with the storms. There is no other option.

Over a decade later when I gave birth to my son, I thought the hate was back to stay. I had so much scar tissue from the damage you caused that the doctor had to physically assist my body in stretching to give birth. They gave me drugs, and they reached into my private place to help my scarred flesh do what should've been natural. I hated you more that day than any other day in my life. You should never have been a thought on the most victorious day of my life, but then again, if not for you, I could've carried more babies in my body. The others didn't survive in the scarred place you created inside me.

Of course, I hated you a lot of other days, too. I hated you when I looked over my shoulder in my own house, when I woke from nightmares, when I was coming down off a high. I did a lot of stupid things in the years between the rape and the version of me I became so I could be able to be a mom.

"I didn't cope well with what happened." That's the sentence

I still use a lot. It's a *safe* sentence that covers drugs, anorexia, dangerous men, and workaholic tendencies. If I use the other sentences, the detailed ones here, people look at me differently. They don't see the woman with an amazing career who put herself through college and grad school. They don't see the person I made. They see you. Even as I type these words, even as I think back on the ugliness over the years, *that's* the part that makes me want to scream.

Your choices that day change how people see me. Far too often when people hear what you did, I stop being a person, a successful businesswoman, and I become a "victim." I sugarcoat the words I use to say I'm a rape survivor so I can avoid their looks, their pity, their sympathy. I don't want a second of sympathy. I want others to simply acknowledge that what I did, how I survived, how I made myself into a successful, stable woman is a hell of a lot more important than what *you* did.

I test people. I bring rape up at some point, bluntly, before I let anyone too close. If I tell them that I was broken, will they still see *me* or will they see you? A lot of people fail the test. I see the pity and other emotions I don't want. I don't want their sorrow or horror. I want them to see *me*. I want them to be happy for me because I'm alive and mostly together.

I never thought I would reach this place, be successful, have a family. I thought you stole all of that. I fought hard—against myself and against my utterly deadly coping mechanisms—to reach this place. So when I tell people I'm a "rape survivor," I'm saying "I *survived*." That is a thing to be proud of. It shouldn't make them give me pity eyes. If they do, it's the first word they hear—*rape*. It's *your act* they hear. If they see *me,* they hear the second word—*survivor*. The latter are the people I trust. They see the victory, not the bleeding.

At the end of everything, what I want you, what I want them, what I want myself to see is that I am strong. What was done *to* me matters less that what *I chose* to do. I chose to be strong. It's not the rape, but the surviving and eventually thriving that matters.

Melissa

FIGHT FOR YOURSELF

Melissa, this powerful piece about the things you haven't said is the namesake for this book. It makes me wonder, when you first shared your experience, did the person hear you? Believe you? Support you?
I told a priest, and he absolutely did not hear me. He knew my rapist, and he relayed *his* side of the story—that my rapist wanted to "do right" by me, be in my life, and so on. It was devastating. Later, I told a second priest—without providing details of the rapist—and *his* response was to ask "how I had offended G-d." These two men were ultimately why I started looking closer at the faith that I'd been raised in since birth and why I left the church.

Did you eventually find a person who did hear you?
For years, I think it was more about speaking so others don't feel silenced. I did my graduate thesis on rape narratives. I speak openly about it. I wrote a novel, *Ink Exchange,* with a rape survivor. I did this essay. It wasn't about finding a single person. There were people. Other survivors. Friends. Lovers. There were plenty of people who didn't make me feel silenced or ashamed.

How long did it take to recover?
I'm not sure how one defines "recovered." I think the major events in our lives change us indelibly. Rape is, obviously, such an event. There are ways that I see the world and people differently, as I talk about in my essay. That's not a failure to recover. It's a realization that these scars are a factor in how I interact with others.

In very literal terms, I was diagnosed with PTSD, in part because of the rape and in part because of things that happened in my life after the rape when I was making some bad choices. Bad choices lead to worse events sometimes, and the cycle is dangerous. So I'm not sure recovery is a state like the end of a race. I don't make those bad choices now, so in that way, I am recovered. In other ways, the PTSD is still very present sometimes, so I don't know if that ever fully resolves. I'd like it to, but I also accept that this is my "new normal" and am fine with it. I survived, and I'm not trying to destroy myself. That, to me, is more than enough of a recovery to celebrate.

Do you mind if we talk about bad choices? How did you break the cycle of anorexia, drugs, and dangerous men?

Honestly? I became a mother. I didn't do it for a solution. I'd had a miscarriage, and to be honest, that child could have belonged to several people, including a drug dealer I had dated for almost two years. A couple of months later, I suddenly had a child growing in my body, and *his* daddy—a US Marine—had a four-year-old. Then I had an infant son and a five-year-old daughter all at once. I couldn't let myself falter. No bad men. No drugs. No cigarettes even. Remember to eat well because it sets an example. Admittedly, I struggle still, especially with the food, but I must succeed because my children require that of me.

How about the workaholic tendencies you mention?

I'm working on it. In 2016, I sold or gave away 75 percent of my belongings and moved to a little house in the desert, specifically so I could slow down. I didn't write as much, and I didn't travel as much. I exercised a lot more. However, I'm doing the writer-in-residence thing, and I teach beginners historical swordfighting, and I co-own a convention. So, I haven't succeeded at slowing down as much as I had hoped. I'm still a work in progress.

That said, I observe Shabbat most weeks, and I'm steadily working toward conversion. Finding my way to the right faith for me has been huge. Judaism has been completing what motherhood began for me: I feel whole and healed more since making the choice to get back on the path to conversion, which I had been considering in my twenties. I think all of the rest—sex, drugs, bad choices, working too much—was trying to fill something. Being with my kids or in prayer gives me peace in a way none of the rest did.

If you don't mind discussing it, when the assault happened, did you know right away it was rape?

There was no way to doubt it. I was in a bit of shock, admittedly. He played a song for me and sang to me while I sat there curled around myself—dressed by then—and shivered. He kissed me good-bye. It was harder in some ways than the physical part. His version of what he'd done was not mine. I was bruised, bleeding, and afraid, and he sang to me. That was the moment of questioning myself. In the rape,

I knew. When I saw the bruises on me or spoke to my doctor or had months of sickness because of the damage, I knew, but there was a very surreal window when my mind wanted to accept his reality.

So, his reality was that the encounter had been consensual? Do you think he has ever realized he is a rapist?
Oh, I doubt that he has ever realized it. His drug use and my being a virgin meant that he wrote off the violence. He told people we had been "together," so when I had some complications that meant I didn't have my cycle for four to five months, people assumed I was pregnant. People talked. He heard and proposed to me. He wanted to "raise our baby together." When I repeatedly insisted I wasn't pregnant, the rumors were that I'd miscarried. That's his narrative. I'd see him for years afterward, and he had a strange tenderness toward me because of "our lost baby." I attributed it to his drug abuse and denial, and he went with the idea that the loss of our child was too traumatic for me. In his version of reality, it wasn't because of what *he* did that I was unwilling to be around him; it was the loss of a baby . . . and no amount of saying I had never been pregnant mattered.

Who helped you the most, or the most effectively, during this time?
Honestly? I was the most effective help. I was also the worst. Getting better isn't some gift or skill that others give you. It's on you. Ultimately, in the dark hours when you are afraid or determined to do something stupid to prove you are okay or even just caught in a nightmare or . . . well, faced with trying to be intimate with someone you love, the only person you can count on to truly let you move on is *you*. No one else sees those nightmares, or has to check your windows three times each before sleep can come. No one else can feel that moment where the memories threaten to replace the present touch. It's on you. So, I think that the best, most reliable person was me. It had to be. Others can listen, share stories, and give you advice, but at the end of it all, the survivor is her or his best advocate and strongest ally.

If you could give a piece of advice to a teen or kid in the same situation, what would it be?

Don't give up on yourself. There are going to be days or nights or moments that suck. There are. It's a fact. However, there are going to be brilliant ones, too. Those good ones are worth weathering the shitty ones. I promise you that. I have stood on a ledge considering death, and I have taken drugs and been falling down drunk and wandered off with criminals of the violent sort. *None* of that dulled the pain. The only way through it is time and belief in yourself. You *can* overcome. It will change you, but change is inevitable. Something awful happened, but if you are alive, you have a shot at amazing future experiences. Don't let the rapist defeat you by giving up on those. He took something from you, but the rest is *yours,* so cling to that, fight for it, and if you falter, *get back up*. It's hard, and a few times that I fell were very much of the lucky-to-be-alive-now variety, so I get that it's hard. And people might be judgmental asses about it, but I swear to you that the only way to truly lose is to stop fighting for yourself. So fight, even if that fight is just small choices. All of the small ones add up over time.

MELISSA TODAY

Melissa Marr is best known for her internationally bestselling *Wicked Lovely* series (HarperCollins) and her children's Norse mythology series, *The Blackwell Pages* (Hachette). Additionally, she is the editor of several fantasy anthologies, and she has just released her debut picture book, *Bunny Roo, I Love You* (Penguin Books). Her books have been published in twenty-eight languages and have been bestsellers in numerous countries. Prior to being a writer, Melissa taught university literature and gender studies. She is the mother to three children: an adult daughter (for whom *Wicked Lovely* was written), a teenager (for whom the Norse books were written), and a toddler (for whom *Bunny Roo* was written).

FINDING WHAT'S GOOD
By BRYSON MCCRONE

The showerhead had broken a long time ago and nobody had come to fix it. A steady jet of water pummeled loudly against the back corner. I was deaf to it. What had happened the hour before started a roar in my head that would not quiet.

It was quick, like ripping off a band-aid. And just as satisfying. That's the part that messed me up; the part that didn't make any sense, then or now.

I'm not that kind of guy, said the fisherman. *I wouldn't do it bare.*

It was then I knew it was going to happen. It's so easy to say you'll fight when it's not happening to you. But then it was happening to me. And I locked up. My bones had all linked together and I was still. I became an object. I remember lying there on my stomach, my face hanging off the bed. I blinked and blinked, hoping that the scene would change. But it didn't.

Looking back, I wonder why my body reacted the way it did. I had been petrified. My body played dead like a possum.

Why did my body betray me?

He wasn't big and strong, or shrimpy and little. He was a boy with a tattoo of a fish hook on his wrist and a face that looked nothing like the one I'd seen on Grindr.

I had never enjoyed sex before. The anticipation was always so much better than the action. At least I knew they were enjoying it when they made noises.

He was silent when he did it.

Sounds were my solace; now I wondered what the point of it was if he didn't at least enjoy what he was taking.

It was my mistake, of course, for thinking that this could have gone the way it *should* have gone. So what if he didn't look the same? I was lonely, and we didn't plan on doing anything besides talk.

But I guess my words got twisted. "Talking" meant something altogether different to him.

When it was over, my body felt as relaxed and woozy as it did after all the consensual sex I'd had. But in my head everything was fuzzy, and I was sweltering hot. I unconsciously knew something was wrong.

I told the boy to leave and he did. It was the only request he seemed okay with following. I took the knife from the kitchen and hid it under my bed, whether for me or another man, I didn't know.

I did not want to have sex with him. But I did, or at least, my body did. I trained myself to believe that it was consensual. It didn't hurt, I didn't *actually* say no, or maybe I did. I couldn't remember. I even climaxed.

All of the signs were there, plain as day.

I saw myself as a victim who did all the wrong things. I was the one who had been baited and hooked. All the clues were there: the false pictures, the way he made himself so comfortable in a strange place, how he kissed me and I kissed back because I felt like that was what I was supposed to do.

Depression hit me hard. I relapsed into self-harming. I found myself in a lot of places I didn't know I could go—in reality and in my head. I also found myself between pages of a tiny little book by Chris Prentiss called *Zen and the Art of Happiness*.

I was with my partner in a local Barnes & Noble when I saw the book sitting on the shelf. It was so small. I picked it up. A tiny Buddha is pictured on the cover, fat and smiling, like happiness was the only thing he'd ever known. I wasn't spiritual or religious, but I was damn sure I wanted to be *just* like that. The ache of being constantly depressed, and feeling as though being assaulted defined everything, exhausted me to no end. It was time to say enough was enough.

When I found myself with Prentiss's book, I found this line: "Everything that happens to me is the best possible thing that can happen to me." Don't jump on the meaning of that just yet. My first instinct was to call bullshit. But the more I read the book, the more I realized the phrase was not something to take *literally*. It was a way of *thinking*.

I knew that being assaulted was one of the worst things that could have happened to me, and for a long time it never felt like that would be an untruth. I wondered how thinking of every experience I had was the best thing that could have happened. Outright, I resented it. What good had come out of all the bad things I had gone through?

It had been about a year after my assault that I found *Zen and the Art of Happiness*. I had time to process everything. I grew mentally and emotionally. I realized that Prentiss's phrase was not meant to be taken outright. It wasn't a mind-set that reflected on the present moment. At least, that's the way I saw it. You had to look from a distance. So, I took a step back and looked at my assault. It was impossible to find something good that came out of it.

Except . . . there was.

I am a writer. I have always been one. When my friend emailed me about this anthology, I decided that I would use my voice. As a queer, cis male, I want to shine light on other survivors in those communities, too. I choose to no longer be silent. I choose to make good of what has happened because I have the power to. The opportunity to share my experience in this book is the good that came out of what happened to me.

Being assaulted is a horrible, horrible thing, but it has also given me an unusual sort of strength I never knew I could possess. It took time and *so* much effort to find that strength. I did not ask for it, but now I have one of the most beautiful gifts to give: the ability to say *I know. I understand. You have the power to be okay.*

BRYSON UNFILTERED
THERE WILL ALWAYS BE HAPPINESS

Bryson, you express a lot of self-blame in this piece—that you had somehow missed the clues, that you didn't fight, and so on. Can you talk more about the complexity of these emotions? When did you realize it was actually rape?

I always knew, subconsciously. I texted a friend the same night it happened and said, "I was just raped." But it didn't feel real. It wasn't until a few weeks later when another friend called me and said it out loud. She knew I was denying it, which was only inhibiting my healing process. My friend is an advocate for rape survivors, so when she said it, I didn't feel like there was any way to deny it anymore. I'd felt somewhat educated on the subject, but she helped me realize that my body's reaction during the assault was not validation for consent.

Many rape myths in our society condition us to misunderstand the complexities of rape, and your piece expresses that complexity. For instance, there was no physical violence—in the way that most imagine it—but there also was no consent. Do you think that the perpetrator considers himself a rapist?
No, I don't think that he does. This is why education in consent is so important.

You say that books and writing helped in the aftermath of the assault. What else was helpful?
A few months after my assault, I met my partner. He knew everything about me, and he was there for me anytime flashbacks froze me. It wasn't just having someone so supportive there, it was also having a positive male figure in my life. He let me take all the time I needed, mentally, physically, and sexually. That was the most comfort I had felt after my assault.

Is it fair to say that there seem to be fewer resources and more stigma for male survivors?
Definitely, and that's why the opportunity to be included in this book is such a blessing.

Were there any male-specific resources that you found useful?
I never really found anything. For me, the most helpful thing is to, when you're ready, listen to other survivors and share your story. This book has been so helpful, too. It shows that people care about what we have been through and what we have to say.

Beyond your contribution here, do you think you will ever write about this experience in a novel or memoir of your own?
Before I was assaulted, I wrote a book about a male survivor of sexual assault. So essentially I already have. That book never got

published, and now that I've lived what my main character did, I'm grateful it didn't. I see so much naïveté in that novel, clichés too, even with all the research I did. One day I will revisit it and do it more justice.

One last question. Have you mastered the art of happiness?
I don't believe it's possible to master happiness. I think the art behind happiness is cherishing it when you feel it and seeing it in the world around you, not just focusing on making your whole life bright and sunny. The fact of life is that you can't always be happy. But there will always be happiness, eventually. I never thought I'd come through my mental illness, but after lots of treatment and a correct diagnosis of bipolar disorder, I have been stable for the last year. And I've been self-harm free for a little bit more than that! This is still something I am "mastering." Remembering those two things always make me happy, even on my worst days.

BRYSON TODAY

Bryson McCrone lives in South Carolina. Aside from personal essay pieces, Bryson also writes novels and poetry.

NEVER STOP REBELLING

By BARBARA MCLEAN

Dear Barbara,

You've just been through something so horrific words cannot
describe it, and I know you are not going to tell anyone for a long
time. Your body has been through a trauma that very few people can
understand. You are very badly bruised, and it's going to be difficult
to hide it, but you will. Understand that you should be in a hospital
right now, and they probably would keep you for several days. You
will never be this physically hurt again in your life. You can actually
use the enforced modesty to make sure nobody sees all the bruises
on your torso. Take care of my beautiful you.

I know that you are battling feelings of guilt and shame because
you believed that your rapist was your boyfriend and that he cared
about you. Make no mistake, he is your rapist. Anytime someone
violently forces you into a sexual situation, it is rape. When someone
holds you down and beats you during a sexual experience, it is rape.
When someone uses you in ways that will only harm and degrade
you, it is rape. Coercion is never foreplay and forcible intercourse—
oral, anal, and vaginal—is always, always rape, without exception.
When he told you that you caused his actions, that is untrue. You
didn't MAKE him do anything. Anything he said after it was over
was bullshit. People do what they want to do.

I know that right now you have a sense of betrayal and feelings
that the people who were tasked to protect you, your parents, didn't
do their job. They're not capable of protecting you, and they will
blame you for their failings. This is going to affect the way you see
love and intimacy for a very long time to come. Your family is also
not going to understand, but you will find allies where you least
expect them. One day, I think in May of your sophomore year, Marie,
that girl who lives over on Central, will walk up to you and ask you
to talk. She will tell you that she was nearly harmed in the same way,
by the same boy. You and she will become friends for the rest of your
life. She will be with you the day you get married. She will be with

you when you have your first child, and she will be the person you call when your mom dies.

You're going to grow into a changing world. People don't see rape the same in 2016 as they do in 1977 and 1978. The world will change. People's beliefs about what constitutes rape will change. Better yet, you're going to be part of that change! You will become an activist and an advocate for the rights of survivors.

However, some things won't change. As far as your parents go, your mother will be cold and judgmental, and your dad will have a very small mind for a long, long time. I'm sorry to say that you can't expect understanding for many years, but it will come and you will be the arbiter of that change. Right now, home is not a happy place, but please know that you are not the problem. They're a mess and it's not your responsibility.

For now, I want you to know a few really important things: YOU are strong, you are positively unbreakable, and although things seem dark, you're gonna pull through. Life will delight and astonish you. You will see beautiful places and have amazing experiences. You will fly on private planes all over the Caribbean; you will go to the shows during New York Fashion Week. You're going to make short films, finish college, and graduate school. But most importantly, you will have two remarkable sons. Those boys will cause you incomparable wonder and raise the bar on how much love you can have for another human being—they will piss you off like nobody else. Cathy, Bridget, and Nancy will give you four beautiful nieces and five nephews, each completely different from the next, and you will adore every one of them.

You will become an accomplished woman: interesting, smart, funny, charming, sexy, and sophisticated . . . yup, yes you, you really will. You will have your watercolor paintings of the ocean exhibited, you'll be a remarkable cook, have a lovely home, coach little league, watch all kinds of sports, and travel. You will see fantastic places, cities so majestic they will make you gasp, and caves on the beaches of Virgin Gorda, with rocks the colors of the rainbow. Remember, I'm the fifty-three-year-old you, and I was there when it happened, so please, please be patient with yourself.

I can't change the past, and surprisingly, I wouldn't if I could. What I would do, if I could, is take the pain away. I would do that in a minute. But sitting where I am nearly forty years later, you're going to come to own this experience, without shame. What will happen is that you will become part of the movement. You'll become a warrior for others and work to help survivors heal and tell their stories. Trust and believe, there will be hope and healing, and after you heal yourself, you will go one step further. You will bring your healing to others, and it will bring you a great sense of purpose and make you feel whole. Most of all, you will be happy. You will be a happy woman.

All the love in the world,
Barbara McLean

BARBARA UNFILTERED
THEN AND NOW

Barbara, why did you choose to keep your experience a secret at the time? Why did you choose not to go the police?
There are so many answers to that question. The first answer is because, in 1977, if you knew your rapist, it wasn't rape. Second, I knew my parents would not support me, and I was correct in that assumption. I can also attribute my reluctance to shame and my inability to accept that I deserved justice. I don't believe that anyone in my position, in 1977, would have gone to the police.

What about later? When did you finally confide in someone who was helpful to you? Who supported you?
I carried my shame around for a really, very long time. However, four years ago, my friend, who is a police officer, confided in me that his daughter was sexually assaulted. He knew that I was a RAINN volunteer, and he asked if I had any advice about how he could convince her to get some additional help. He told me her story, and then I told him mine, and it was the first time I had spoken to anyone in law enforcement. He told me that if I had gone to the ER or the police with my injuries at the time, they would have believed

me. Despite the fact that I was actually only telling a friend, I felt a significant measure of acceptance and healing.

Can you tell us a little bit about your advocacy work and volunteerism?
My decision to pursue a career in social work has helped me more than anything else. I began by becoming a RAINN speaker between undergrad and graduate school. Then I trained for certification to answer the rape crisis hotline, and I do that two nights a week. When the opportunity to take the class to volunteer as a trauma advocate in the emergency room was presented to me, I didn't hesitate. Then, when there was an opening in their Violence Intervention and Treatment Program, they just gave me the job, and here I am.

You are clearly very good at what you do. As someone who helps survivors directly, if you could change one policy regarding how sexual assaults are handled, what would it be?
I wrote my thesis on the value of second responders. I believe that rape survivors need a reliable second responder to be with them in the ER, to help them interact with law enforcement and the justice system, and to assist them in obtaining the follow-up care that could be vital in terms of recovery. Eventually, I would like to have my own agency and provide that type of service.

In your piece, you mention how differently rape is perceived today than it was in the past. In your experience, what has changed for the better?
People have realized that the old adages, such as "boys will be boys," are excuses that enable rapists to commit crimes that they will never be punished for. The onus of being sexually assaulted on a date or by a friend is no longer placed solely on the woman. Those who rape, no matter what the context may be—including marriage and prostitution—can be held accountable for their actions. Those who stand by and watch are taken to task for their inaction.

That's heartening. What still needs work?
Some things haven't changed, especially when it comes to sexual assault. There are still salacious stories in the news of victims who lured their abusers to commit rape. Law enforcement and the legal system still experience inertia when dealing with sexual assault

cases, and perpetrators do horrible things and still only receive a slap on the wrist as punishment.

If the incident you experienced happened today instead of in the 1970s, do you think you would report it?
Yes, I think I would report it. I think I would have confidence that it's okay to stand up for myself and protect myself. I believe that I would go to the hospital and take the time to make sure that I was okay. I think younger women now understand the value of caring for themselves, in putting their needs first, as opposed to how they did in 1977. With the ongoing destigmatization, I think, generally, younger women are stronger in these situations than they used to be.

BARBARA TODAY

Barbara McLean hid the injuries from a childhood sexual assault for many years and, as an adult, became involved in an abusive relationship. Eventually, Barbara enrolled in a master's program to study social policy with the desire to change how sexual assault survivors perceive themselves. Today, she works for a Violence Intervention and Treatment Program in Brooklyn, New York, and she volunteers on a sexual assault hotline as well as in a local emergency room. These services provide critical support for survivors who need a safe place to talk about what happened.

THE INTERROGATION ROOM
By STEPHANIE OAKES

They led me into an interrogation room. At least that's what it looked like to me at eight years old. The room was windowless and gray-painted, a table at the center, and it looked exactly like the kind of room where bad guys are questioned by cops with shiny badges, who you know are good because they're handsome and clean. There were a couple of exceptions:

No mirrored-glass wall behind which other cops could listen in, like I'd seen in a million police procedural TV shows.

The presence of a white piece of paper on the tabletop, a blunt-bordered anatomical sketch of a girl's body printed on it.

And, lastly, the fact that the person sitting opposite the cops wasn't a criminal. It wasn't a master thief, or a spousal abuser, or a murderer.

It was me.

***

For me, there's the event—the assault, the rape—and there's everything after. What hurt worse? By far, the everything after. That might not be something people realize. My rape wasn't particularly violent, at least not in the way I was trained to think about rape. No dark alley, but instead my own backyard. No physical wounds, though plenty of the other kind. And the rapists weren't even strangers with weapons, but fourteen-year-old neighborhood boys that I'd grown up around.

What followed, though, was every kind of violence. The shame, knocking me around like a Golden Gloves boxer. The blame and self-hatred that filled my lungs without my even realizing, like some kind of odorless poison. Among my family, I stepped around the word *rape* like it was a mine that could blow us all up.

And there was that interview with the police.

***

The police officers were men, two of them. In my memory, I have no sense of the time that was involved in their questioning, but I left the room afterward feeling exhausted and pummeled. The policemen were brutal, direct, unsympathetic, and they spoke to me as if I had done the wrong thing, not the neighbor boys. This was not what I had been expecting—I'd seen the way victims are questioned on TV. They get sympathy and arm pats and time to cry and be heard. Instead, the policemen peppered me with their gruff-voiced demands of *Tell us what happened*, and *What was your role in the events?* I felt astonished and knocked off my moorings.

My parents waited out in the tense, antiseptic waiting room. The policemen didn't allow them into the room while I was questioned. I learned later that they thought I'd be less forthcoming with information if my parents were beside me. Maybe that's true, but it also allowed the cops to question me more relentlessly than they probably would have if my parents were there.

I remember how fixated the officers were on something that hadn't even happened—the idea that I had received something in exchange for what the boys had done to me. *What was it? Was it money? Was it a toy? Was it a book? If it was money, how much money? Forty dollars? Twenty? We heard that it was twenty. Are you saying you were lying earlier? What is the truth, Stephanie?*

Though the police didn't tell me so much in their words, I could decipher the truth in their tensed shoulders, in their downturned mouths: They didn't believe me.

I was a shy kid. Maybe my answers were less than direct. Maybe my voice was quiet and weak. Maybe my embarrassment looked to them like a child who's been caught in a lie. And perhaps the officers were thinking about how the boys' parents were breathing down their necks, making *their* voices heard. I found out later that one of the boys' mothers had called my mom, scolding her for going straight to the police, for not "handling it between neighbors."

Her son had been subjected to brutal police questioning, she said. Did my mom have any idea what that was like for a child? Sometimes I wonder if there is real evil in the world. And I wonder if evil is moments like that. Sanctimonious, neighborly, defending the indefensible.

Her son had lied and was believed. I told the truth and was not.

I've started to think about the way I was taught about sexual assault. I remember once in second grade, our teacher stood in the front of the classroom and discussed an assortment of taboo topics: alcohol, cigarettes, crime. This must have been part of a required life skills curriculum. The students listened attentively, little jaws hanging slightly open.

My teacher held up a shadowbox with rows of colorful pills lined up inside and told us never to eat anything like them because they could be *drugs*. She told us not to let anyone touch us because that could be *rape*. The words *drugs* and *rape* seemed to go hand-in-hand. I could tell they were things that only happened to bad people. It was something that you chose. I swept them away in my mind. I was good, I told myself. I would never do drugs, and I would never be raped.

The next year, though, I was raped. I didn't know at the time that I'd been raped exactly, not until years later when, with shaking fingers, I typed the sentence "What is rape?" into a search engine. But I knew that what I'd allowed to happen was wrong—my teacher had told me so. And the police had echoed it.

***

All my life, I had longed to please the adults around me. Here I was, telling the truth, and the answers were not to their satisfaction. In that police interrogation room, this was the day when the first, early seedling of shame was planted within me.

I completely understand how interrogation techniques can break people down, can plant false memories, can make them admit to crimes they haven't committed. By the end, I felt like a criminal. I still knew the truth of what had happened to me, but I also knew that the police didn't believe me.

The boys were not prosecuted.

***

How to describe the feeling of not being believed?

It is the feeling of disappearing.

Feeling myself fade away into invisibility, every cell shrinking in on itself. Feeling like I should apologize though I'd done nothing wrong. Hearing, loud as church bells, the tacit statement that, "You are telling the truth, yet to us you are nothing but a liar."

***

After the interview, one of the policemen led me to a closet full of sad-looking stuffed animals and toys. A strange kind of token for what I'd endured. I remember observing the dark closet for a long time, the wooden shelves scattered with donated toys. There was a monkey with a scary plastic face and cymbals in its hands. I didn't choose the monkey, but for some reason it sticks in memory more than the toy I actually took.

There's something so gut-punchingly sad about that closet of toys. That it needed to exist at all. That it probably still does.

There were odd, discordant moments like that sprinkled throughout the aftermath of my rape. The closet of stuffed animals, the cat posters plastered on the walls of a medical clinic where I underwent what I now know was a rape kit procedure. Those stupid, material gifts had been placed there by adults with the express purpose of helping children survive the experience of rape.

But none of it made anything even a fraction better. Even as I considered the choice of stuffed animal carefully, like it mattered, I knew that something was very wrong. The act of playing along by taking a toy reassured the adults more than it helped me. The stuffed animals and the posters were stand-ins for the words I needed to hear, the things that, for some reason, I've learned it is so difficult for people to say to rape victims.

Sometimes, I imagine walking into that police precinct, pushing the door to that interrogation room open, kneeling down in front of my eight-year-old self, and pronouncing, clear-eyed, "I believe you," and "None of this was your fault." And I'd say it again and again until it stuck.

***

STEPHANIE UNFILTERED
IT WASN'T YOUR FAULT

Stephanie, your experience with law enforcement was a veritable disaster, and I am so sorry it happened. What are your thoughts today on that encounter?

I've spent a great deal of time considering why the police handled my situation like they did. I've looked up pictures of myself at that age and wondered how their reaction to that girl—shy, scared, and so young—could've been so breathtakingly unsympathetic. I've done some research about how the police handle the sexual assault of children. One of the more interesting things I learned about was the McMartin Preschool trial, the most expensive and lengthy trial in American history. In 1983, employees at a preschool in a wealthy community in California were accused of sexual abuse. The trial was built on the taped testimony of hundreds of children. However, when those tapes were analyzed, it was determined that the techniques counselors and law enforcement used to produce those stories of abuse were coercive. The interviewers asked leading questions and repeated questions over and over until the children changed their answers. The interviewers would often suggest scenarios of abuse that, at the end of lengthy and arduous interviews, the children would agree had happened. The tapes were thrown out as evidence, all the preschool employees were acquitted, and the local police department and prosecutors were publicly disgraced.

I wondered if there were ripple effects of that event that were being felt when my case made it to the local police department about a decade later. Sometimes, I imagine that, after the McMartin Preschool trial, a memo with the words "Don't believe children when they say they've been raped" was passed around to every police department in the country. I can't help but wonder if the McMartin Preschool trial influenced the methods used for questioning me, and likely all children who entered that room with stories of sexual abuse.

Can you tell us more about what happened after the interrogation? Were charges pressed? Was there a follow-up?

My understanding is that nothing happened. There wasn't enough evidence to bring charges against the boys. I remember hearing that the result of the medical exam I underwent was inconclusive, meaning there was no evidence of an assault. And there was no follow-up. A counselor advised my parents not to mention it to me because there was a chance I wouldn't remember it happened. If I could pinpoint the single worst thing to have happened in all of this, it might be that advice. It turned my experience into a secret. It meant that I had to deal with the memory all alone. My family didn't know until much later that, during all of the years when I was silent about what happened to me, I was living in turmoil. I believed what had happened was my fault.

This story conveys your intense feeling of isolation. Your agency was taken away by multiple people. What do you think people could have done better—such as your parents, the police, emergency workers, and teachers?

I wish my parents had insisted on being in the room while I was questioned. Nobody in my family had encountered the police beyond being pulled over for speeding, so I think they genuinely didn't understand their rights or mine. They trusted the police, and they didn't know that they could demand to be with me while I was questioned.

I would also advise parents to make sure their child has someone to talk to about what happened to them (either the parents themselves or a therapist). The alternative—silence and secrecy—is beyond harmful. Secrets are poisonous. Secrets breed shame. As an adult, I went to therapy for the first time. I hadn't spoken about my assault since that interview with the police. The years of silence had made it so difficult to talk about, I felt like I was dragging the words out of my throat. It was one of the most terrifying experiences I can recall. And I feel like it could have been prevented had I been given more opportunities to speak about what happened to me.

As for the police, I understand that they are in a difficult spot when, for whatever reason, doubt has been cast on a sexual assault victim's story. But even if they are certain that the victim is lying—as seems to be the case with the police who interviewed me—they can be wrong. It's important for police to understand that they can cause more harm and sow more shame in their questioning than even the original assault. There has to be a way to treat a victim differently to the way a criminal is treated.

The women who conducted my medical exam were extremely kind and efficient. I think, under the circumstances, that's the ideal situation for something so vile. I wish that, though the exam showed that there was no medical evidence of a rape, that someone had assured me that that didn't mean I was a liar. That my experience was not invalidated by the results.

I'm a teacher now, and I've observed firsthand that rape culture can be present in schools just as it is everywhere else. I would hope that antiquated ideas about rape—such as what I experienced in second grade—have died out, but I know they probably haven't. I wish consent was part of every health curriculum, and that the teachers who teach those classes were better trained. I hope teachers are strong enough to correct their colleagues who may be spreading harmful misinformation.

What about peers? Were your friends or classmates aware of the situation?
My classmates weren't aware of what happened to me. It was such a secret in my family that I didn't speak about it to friends until into my twenties. I believe it was never a story that got beyond our family and the families of the boys who perpetrated the rape. Sexual assault was rarely mentioned in school, except as a cautionary tale and a way to police girls. I had absorbed certain "truths" back then that I can't even recall where I originally learned them—it's the girl's responsibility to not be raped; girls who behave well don't get raped—but it must've been in the air while I was in middle school and high school. The kind of thing you absorb unconsciously that shapes your worldview and makes unlearning self-hatred so difficult.

Was there a person who helped you the most?
Since sexual assault was such an unspoken topic in my real life, the internet was the first place I found understanding about what had happened to me. I had never heard the terms "victim blaming" or

"rape culture" in my normal life. It was the internet that gave me the tools I needed to stop blaming myself. The first incident I remember vividly was in 2012, when the internet was furiously discussing the Steubenville rape case. It's such a disheartening, horrifying story. However, the conversations happening on my Twitter and Tumblr feeds, the universal outrage and disgust, were somehow validating. Our shared anger also gave me the opportunity to be angry about my own assault, something I hadn't really processed before.

What would you like to say to a teen or kid in your situation?
You're allowed to be angry about what happened to you. In fact, it might be very important for you to be angry for a while. And it really, really was not your fault.

STEPHANIE TODAY

Stephanie Oakes is a teacher and YA author from Washington State. Her debut novel, *The Sacred Lies of Minnow Bly* (Dial/Penguin, 2015), about a girl who escapes from a religious commune only to find herself at the center of a murder investigation, is based on the Grimm fairy tale "The Handless Maiden." Her second YA mystery is *The Arsonist* (Dial/Penguin, 2017).

LITTLE GIRLS
By LARENA PATRICK

We moved around a lot. Not because one of my parents was in the military or had a job that necessitated transfers. It was because I had a very unstable childhood thanks to my stepfather, who in addition to being abusive, was a drug addict. Despite the fact that we were then a family of nine, he didn't consider anyone's interests but his own, and whenever a reason or whim arose, we were headed someplace else. We would suddenly be moving house with no warning. I don't remember ever living more than two years in one place until I got to high school. By then, I had gone to six different schools. So nearly every year I was the new girl—forced to quickly catch up and get acquainted with my peer group, many of whom knew each other for years already.

One year stands out. I was in fifth grade. We had moved once again, and I remember my first day at my new school when I met a girl who immediately took it upon herself to make introductions. Tracy Miller. She had such an authentic and sweet smile. I loved that she seemed oblivious about the fact that her front teeth were slightly buck and crooked. She smiled without a bit of self-consciousness. Her hair was the opposite of mine: long, light brown, perfectly straight with bangs. Nothing like the curly, soft afro of mine that my mother insisted on taming into braids. She wouldn't let me leave the house without braids and barrettes in my hair, but Tracy never wore any adornments, not even ribbons like most of us girls did. Now here was this crooked-toothed, bright-eyed girl talking to me. Making an effort to welcome me into the class.

Surely, I couldn't trust that she had a genuine desire for friendship. I'm sure I wasn't that interesting. I almost didn't know if I could take her seriously. Besides, I wasn't about to invest that much time into really getting to know her. It was pointless, since my family would probably move again without warning, and there would go another year spent making a friendship that would abruptly end when I was whisked away to another school without even having a chance to say good-bye.

But here we were, for now, sitting in class. She, this friendly, helpful girl who seemed to sincerely desire a friendship with me, the new girl, who had to learn all about these kids and this school. I was just a quiet, slightly nerdy girl. I cautiously accepted her cheerful kindness, maintaining my typical reserved response. I reacted that way to everyone—reserved. Not shy. See, in my mind, being "shy" has a connotation of being nervous or fearful. I wasn't nervous about meeting people; I was strategically cautious. If anyone actually knew what I had lived through by the age of ten, they certainly wouldn't call me fearful.

But Tracy and that smile, the deep soul that I could see in her bright blue eyes, made me trust her, even want her as my friend. It was easy to like her. We soon discovered a mutual love for animals. I wasn't allowed to have pets, so I got to experience them vicariously through Tracy. She had a cool-looking orange cat that she loved. I would ask her every day how Morris was doing, and she would show me photos and tell me stories. That love and affection for animals sealed the deal. She and I officially became "best friends forever." But we only got to talk at school because I wasn't allowed to invite anyone home, nor was I allowed to go to anyone's house. Those were my stepfather's rules. So we had to relegate our friendship to the hours that we could actually see each other, 8 a.m. to 2:30 p.m., Monday to Friday.

It probably was a good thing that neither Tracy nor I went to each other's homes. I now speculate that the possibility of our childhood traumas actually could have been compounded had either of us been in each other's houses. Tracy lived with three brothers and her dad. She was the only girl. Her mom was gone. I don't remember the story about her mom, whether she left them, remarried, or passed away. And although my mom was not "gone," often she was. She was either just going to work as I was getting in from school or sleeping during the day after working a night shift. I didn't get to spend much time with her at all. And at ten, many girls still want their moms around. I certainly did, and even though she didn't say it often, Tracy did, too. In many ways our lives were parallel.

Tracy and I made the most of school hours to nurture our friendship. In addition to being animal lovers, we were both active and loved to play outside. We enjoyed many of the playground games, such as dodgeball and four square, and could play them just as well as the boys who thought they ran the blacktop. In the classroom, we kept up the grade school fun by passing notes. It helped that we sat in the back of the class, next to each other. It made the note passing, this precious girl bonding, a bit easier.

We wrote about the usual fifth-grade topics: who tried to get us out in dodgeball, her cat's antics, and which boys were maybe just a little bit cute. We shared our likes and dislikes and classroom gossip. I'm not sure who initiated it or what inspired the shift, but eventually, our notes became drawings. These were comic-like drawings separated into boxes that told a story with stick figures acting out vignettes in each little box.

And then it happened.

One day, we were alternating drawing on a note and exchanged it back and forth. One of us started it and passed it. The other added to it and passed it back. We kept this up for several turns. This wasn't about playground games or our classmates. I read her additions and she read mine. And suddenly, after looking at the explicit drawings that had materialized on the page, we both knew.

It was a moment that will, likely, stay with me for the rest of my life. For seconds we looked into each other's eyes and knew and could say without uttering a syllable: *You're being molested at home just like I am!* That revelation is flash-frozen into my memory. In that moment, time stopped.

We didn't say a word to each other. I didn't ask her, and she didn't ask me, but we knew. We knew that we truly *were* living parallel lives. Looking at the images on that note, the childish yet descriptive drawings, could only mean that we had experienced things that no ten-year-olds should know about.

We must have been caught up in the moment—silently connecting over this profound connection and new, deeper level to our friendship—because that was the moment that we got busted for passing notes in class. Our teacher walked up behind us undetected, and he wasn't content to just have us toss out our note and continue with the lesson, which usually happened when other kids were caught with notes. For some reason—perhaps he saw over our shoulders a glimpse of what we had drawn—he insisted that we give the paper to him. He took the note and left us with a mutual feeling of horrified embarrassment and panic! This page filled with drawings inappropriate for children was about to be seen by an adult. I realized I would surely be punished, but I also thought: Maybe this disclosure would inspire some investigation by the authorities and finally set us both free from our abusive households. I was definitely mortified that anyone was seeing our note, but this could be freedom. I could be taken away to the safety of a foster home. Or better yet, my stepfather would finally be hauled off to prison for the crime of what he was doing to me. I would finally be validated and protected.

Apparently, I was hoping for too much. No such thing happened. No social worker came to visit our house. Nor were the police called. Our teacher sent a copy of the note to each of our parents, and my stepfather was the "parent" who got the photocopy. He reassured the teacher that I would discontinue drawing such things in school. And for some reason the teacher accepted this response.

And, of course, Tracy's only parent was her father, so no doubt he also found a way to diffuse whatever concerns our teacher may have had. I have wondered how that conversation went because she also remained in her home. And that was that. Nothing changed.

Maybe there weren't laws then, in the 1980s, compelling teachers to report suspected abuse to authorities. Maybe it was a result of living in the semi-rural south, where life always tends to move a few years behind the more metropolitan areas, that no one intervened. This teacher had a perfect opportunity to make a difference in the lives of not one but two girls who were obviously being sexually abused, and it was squandered. The "discovery" was sent directly to the place where it would do the least amount of good—home.

If only our teacher had taken the time to really look and listen and talk to us. To ask: "Where did you learn this? Has anyone ever made you do these things? Are you being hurt at home? Are you being made to do things that you don't want to do? I'll protect you. I'll get you help." If someone had thought to say this to me, I would have told them: "Yes, I am being hurt at home. And so is my friend."

Until the moment when I saw that drawing, I thought I was alone. I didn't think that anyone else could ever know what it was like to hate to have to go home because it was unsafe there. I thought it was just me, a flawed girl who had done something so bad in my young life that I deserved to be abused. I would have never thought that this girl, my adorable best friend, was living through the same thing I was. There was no way that Tracy, this bright-eyed, friendly, always smiling girl deserved to be molested. We were little girls. It took me years to realize and truly know that, despite how I felt then, I didn't deserve to be molested, either. And neither do you.

LARENA UNFILTERED
KNOWING THE SIGNS

Larena, after growing up in an abusive household, did you find your way to recovery?
I wasn't able to start recovery until I was out of the house, in my late teens, and it took several years. In fact, things still occasionally come up for me to address even now. There are days when I feel so removed and strong and like I am remembering some story I read. And some days when I hear something or experience something and I'm completely in tears, remembering that it is my own painful story. So I realize that I am living with the scars that have healed but have the potential to still be triggered. Fortunately, so absolutely fortunately, I am doing my best to not let those painful memories keep me from having an amazing life!

Your story is, in part, about a teacher who missed an opportunity to make a huge difference in your life. I worry that still today people are not aware of the signs and signals of abuse. Of course, your note was an overt sign, but were there other signs people might have noticed?
One thing that I picked up on, even as a ten-year-old, was that Tracy had an uneasiness and a deep sadness in her voice whenever she talked about her family. As a peer, I didn't have the vocabulary or skills to address that with her, but thinking back now, I believe any adult who works with children would and should dig a bit to try to

uncover what those feelings were about. A friend could encourage more sharing and may get a friend to open up. I don't know if I displayed the same sadness, but one thing that stands out for me was the fact that I hated to be hugged or touched by anyone. People would sometimes comment on it, in a way meant to criticize me for it, but no one ever considered there was a serious reason why I was extremely sensitive to being touched. I would say those signs are something worth investigating if ever anyone shows either behavior.

Was justice ever served?
No, justice has not been served. It's a crazy, huge thing, possibly with family drama erupting as I continue to move forward with taking legal steps toward pressing or at least filing charges. It's taken me a while to even get the correct information to know that I can now move ahead with some type of formal police report. So even though it's been years, I'm just starting to move ahead to see what legal recourse I may have.

Now that my stepfather has just died, I'll have to see if it's worthwhile or even possible to continue to file a report that will be on police record. Mainly, I want it to be recorded that this man was a child abuser. Despite what his friends or family may say about him, he was a pedophile and got away with not serving time, but it's on record.

As you work on legal steps, do you find that the system is effective?
I think the justice system has been effective only to a limited degree. In my experience they are so focused on keeping the peace, and coming to some agreement on the spot, they sometimes forget that there is clearly *not* an equal balance of power in domestic situations. In domestic violence, sexual assault, and abuse, there is clearly an advantage of strength and power that the abuser has, and the victim needs to be protected and reassured of her or his safety. There should be, at the time that an officer is called out, options available to the survivors. I feel that there is a lack of empathy for survivors. I would love for law enforcement to learn to listen on a deeper level and be better informed of resources to let the survivor know right away that they have ways of immediately escaping the situation by providing those resources where they exist.

That's a good point. Power seems to play a huge role there. You mention that it would be useful for a survivor to have options. In an ideal world, what would those helpful options or resources for a survivor look like?
I believe that having a center—something akin to a boarding school where youth could go immediately upon being removed from their abusive homes—could be an amazing setting. Someplace that emphasizes healing and continued education and support by trained professionals and peers. This would be absolutely invaluable to a young person who is finally able to escape an abusive situation. This could be permanent or temporary, depending on the legal process and on whether the home becomes a safe place for the young person to return to or not. I also think offering options for learning self-care and different modalities for healing as the survivor begins the healing process would be a great place to start. And schools should know about such safe places for their youth. I haven't heard of anything like this, and I think this could be incredible! Something more supportive and safe than the typical placement in foster homes, which can sometimes be just as bad, if not worse, than the home the survivor was in.

What was the most helpful for you in recovery?
Writing. Definitely. Poetry and writing on my own as a child, expressing emotions on paper that I was forced to suppress helped me, so that by the time I was in therapy, journaling was easy and extremely helpful to me. Drawing also helped and still helps and any other type of artistic expression for me has been great. And having someone listen was probably most helpful.

Victim advocates, which I've just recently contacted again, have been utterly supportive and invaluable in giving me the strength to revisit my experiences and learn that I actually may have more legal recourse than I was initially told years ago. Also, body trauma healing; specifically, the experience of having an incredible Healing Arts retreat with the Joyful Heart Foundation changed my life!

Can you tell us anything about victim advocates? Where do you find them and what do they do?
I was connected to victim advocates through the local police station in my hometown. They are more knowledgeable than the

average police officer about domestic and sexual abuse laws and organizations and when it comes to knowing statute of limitations, if there are any for your state. They also can talk about options beyond pressing charges if there isn't evidence, and in my experience, they are extremely supportive and patient as you work through the emotional process of deciding what legal steps to take. I would suggest asking at your local police station to see if there are such people, who are not part of the department but work with the detectives to help prepare survivors should they decide to pursue legal action.

What would you say to a teen or child in this situation?

I would tell her or him: You are an amazing and incredibly strong person! You are not alone. No matter how lonely, hurt, scared, and angry you may feel, you are not alone and there are people who want to and who will help you. It may take years but learn to trust and love yourself, and please, *please* take all the time you need to heal. Go to therapy. Do the drawings, read the books, cry, dance, write your feelings. Take each day, each moment, one at a time. Imagine what you want your life to be like, and seek the professional and uplifting people who can help you realize that you can have that life of your dreams. And look forward to the day when you can say that you love yourself.

Did you have a positive experience in therapy? Can you tell us a little about it?

Therapy saved my life. Literally. I got so depressed that I was suicidal, and I found some of the best therapists who helped pull me out of that darkness. In those sessions, one of my greatest comforts in dealing with the PTSD that arose from my abuse was being listened to and being allowed to express every single thing that I was feeling. The pain, the rage, the grieving. All of it. I wasn't lectured to. I wasn't told to "get over it." I wasn't told it was too much or too scary for anyone to handle. I was given permission to feel and honestly express everything that came up. Those moments in therapy were priceless. And it's how I'm here today.

Last question: Have you ever tried to reconnect with Tracy?
I have thought about getting in touch with Tracy. In fact, recently, I searched a little on Facebook to see if I could find her, but so far I haven't. We lost touch long ago. Of course, we moved the summer before I started seventh grade, and I haven't talked to her since we were kids.

I would love to know how she got out of the situation and how her life has been since our childhood. I also would want her to know that, even if neither of us knew back then, I believe that moment when I knew that we had both experienced abuse, it somehow made me feel less alone in the world. And that mattered.

I do hope that I can find her one day. I'd love to thank her for being such a good friend.

LARENA TODAY

Larena Patrick has had a varied career path, working for a few years as a teacher and youth director in her early adulthood while living in Virginia. She has spent time volunteering with women's shelters, suicide hotlines, and working to feed and shelter homeless people. Social outreach and working as a social advocate has been important to her, and she is often inspired to find ways of incorporating it into her life and work. She now lives and works in the entertainment industry in Los Angeles as an actor and filmmaker, and she has recently started writing and directing her own projects, most of which spotlight or analyze current social issues or share stories that aren't often given attention. Having an opportunity to share her story with many other writers for this anthology is an honor and absolutely aligned with what she wants to do with her art.

THE LETTER I NEVER SENT
By SHANYN KAY SPRAGUE

Mom,
You were supposed to believe me. You were supposed to shelter
me, guide me, teach me, and care for me. But that day in the garage
you robbed me of nearly all the self-esteem I had managed to
hang on to.

I had already spent so much time coming out of the fog. I spent
months absorbed by self-doubt while trying to piece together a
cold case nearly as old as I was. I sorted out fragments of memories
and obsessed over solving the puzzle.

Puzzle pieces came in the shape of my childhood bedsheets.
The nightlight in my bedroom. His cologne bottle sitting on the
bathroom counter. His cologne . . . that smell which seemed to fill
any space I occupied without a moment's notice. The fragments
haunted me from morning till night. They would leap out of my
unconscious mind and linger for seconds or for minutes before
slipping away again, back into the darkness.

After months of excavating the muddied memories, I saw the
bathtub: my small, naked body sitting on his lap. I felt his touch on
my skin. And as I wrestled with these realizations, these memories,
my life as I knew it unraveled.

He stopped being my dad the moment he decided to touch me;
he stopped being my dad when I was just four years old.

Remember the Father's Day I pulled you into the garage?
It was the only place I knew we wouldn't be overheard, but as I
stood between the washing machine and the car, I realized I was
speaking in a hushed tone, forcing the words out. "I can't do this
today. I think . . . I think he molested me."

Saying the words out loud took more energy and strength than
I thought possible: The words came from my toes—they came
with nerves and muscles dangling off of them—they came up
from the depths of my soul, buried under the heavy silence of the
past fifteen years. The words landed on the cement floor without

a sound. I couldn't look at you, but I could hear my voice shake. I could feel the tears stinging my eyes.

"Do you have proof?" you asked.

"I have my memories," I replied, finally daring to meet your flintlike gaze. But I wondered: *What proof could I provide to this fifteen-year-old crime?* You asked me what I remembered, and I told you. It was still early then and the only complete memory I had was the bath.

"Until you have proof," you informed me, "you need to go in there and pretend like everything is okay." All the wind left my sails. I was defeated, startled, and at a loss for words. Even if I'd been able to muster the energy to fight back, your face told me not to argue.

So I did as you requested: I pretended as best I could.

But you are my mother. You were supposed to believe me. You were supposed to shelter me, guide me, teach me, and care for me. You were supposed to trust me. Instead, you shut me down and turned your back on me.

Sometimes I wonder: If I'd had all the details before I told you—if I'd had more of the memories I have today—if I'd already remembered him raping me—would it have made a difference?

I'm sure your response would have been the same.

Kim and Kristin, mother and daughter, were my rocks during that time. They sat with me in silence and in tears. They listened when I needed to talk and held my hand when I needed consolation. Even when we were three thousand miles apart, Kristin was there for me. I shared my pain and confusion with these women, and in return I was met with belief, love, encouragement, and comfort.

I know you have often wondered why Kim and I are so close. I see you become jealous of her on occasion, even though you've never said it. The answer is simple: Kim was there when you weren't. And while I'm sorry if that hurts you, I am not sorry for the fact that it's true.

She believed me the first time I told her what happened. Sitting in her brightly lit living room covered with antiques, the first words out of Kim's mouth were, "I'm so sorry that happened to you." She told me she knows it's difficult to go through the painful process of remembering. "But," she added, "it's like scooping out the gunk from the inside of a pumpkin: You feel so much better when it's cleaned out and smooth."

You and I have come a long way since that moment in the garage, but we will never be able to go back to what we had before. In the years that followed it, you told me with your words and behavior that you didn't believe me: You didn't believe he had abused me. I know you tried—you tried to take me at my word, but you couldn't. When you looked at me, you saw a liar, and I know that's what you saw because, sometimes, I could see myself through your eyes.

When you finally apologized for not believing me—ten years after my Father's Day confession—it didn't erase the pain. You got your proof when my sister came forward with an account similar to mine. But your apology made the hurt worse. You got your proof, but what did *I* get? Proof I had never been enough. It honestly felt like you believed her more than you had ever believed me. *Why was her word good enough, when mine wasn't?*

There are still days when I am angry with you. There are still days when I am so hurt I can barely breathe. But those days are few and far between. Most days I can accept you for who you are: the good with the bad, the sweet with the bitter.

In recent months, you've said that I am a private person. You've said you want us to be closer. I hear that, but I have to take care of myself now. I need to remain healthy, and that means I need to have boundaries. Please know that I am giving you all I can, even if it may not seem like much to you. I am thirty-three years old now, and I have spent three-quarters of my life in silence: sometimes imposed by myself, sometimes imposed by others, and almost always imposed by fear. I will not be silent anymore. I need you to know that.

Please, don't hold it against me.

Shanyn Kay

_____

HARD CONVERSATIONS

Shanyn, you call your abuse a "cold case" that you had to figure out. How did you come to the realization that you had been sexually abused?
The abuse started when I was four years old. While I instinctually knew it to be wrong, I had no concept of what was happening. I repressed it for over a decade, living and hiding in silence and fear. The memories started surfacing in small ways when I was eighteen, but it wasn't until just after my nineteenth birthday that I started putting the pieces together. The pieces came together with time and therapy, hard work, facing my fears, and trusting myself. When I finally remembered, I was completely retraumatized: I felt like it was happening all over again. It was as though my entire existence had changed. I couldn't even say I had been "sexually assaulted" until twenty-five years after the abuse started.

I will never get back the fifteen years I spent in darkness, but in some ways I am glad it was that way: the repression offered me a certain protection so that I could grow up, grow stronger, grow healthier. Now that I have, I get to protect myself in new ways, I get to help others, and I get to shatter the silence I lived under for so long.

How long did it take to recover? Do you feel that you are fully recovered?
Recovery came in stages for me. Once I knew I had been assaulted, it took about two years before I was functional. But I still struggled often; I still pretended to be normal. I found a better balance once I started to really *work* on healing. And when I started helping others with their recovery, my recovery turned a corner I never saw coming.

This year it will be fifteen years since the memories first began, and last year was the first year that I really felt like the word *recovery* was appropriate for me. I will always be recovering. I don't believe my journey will ever be over, and I don't think I will ever be *over* what happened to me, but I am healthy now. I am standing on my own terms. And I know that when the hard times come again, as I'm sure they will, I will be able to get through them. After all, look how far I've already come!

You found great allies in Kristin and Kim. Can you tell us more about them?

A handful of unexpected people popped into my life and helped me immeasurably, especially when I was first dealing with everything. Over the years, I have managed to thank them. But there has been one person who has stuck by my side longer than any other. My best friend Kristin is the one person who has consistently stayed up late with me when I couldn't sleep, encouraged my hopes, and held me when I was afraid. She has talked me through bad days and listened to me when I was at my wit's end. Kristin has been my confidante and supporter for over twenty years. We always say: "We've done life together." And I am beyond grateful for that fact.

I really love the sentiment of doing life together. Could you talk a little bit more about your mom and the Father's Day confession? After you told your mom, did you ever notice your parents' relationship change?

No, I never saw their relationship change—at least, not in the way I think you are asking this question. However, about a month after I told my mom what happened, my father moved out and filed for a divorce. The reasons were completely unrelated to the abuse. I do not have any kind of relationship with him now.

You mention that you and your mom have come a long way since that day in the garage. What has that been like?

It's been difficult, to say the least! We have certainly come a long way, with many ups and downs. I find, though, that when we have good boundaries with each other, we both do better. In other words, those boundaries allow our time together to be more joyful and our conversations to be more honest. I'm grateful for those moments when we can enjoy each other's company. We are in a good place now, and I hope that we continue to be.

What sort of coping strategies do you have that have worked for you over the years?

Coping strategies vary widely, both from person to person and even within a person. I went through a whole spectrum of strategies myself, but two of the most helpful were art and music. I was drawn to visual art: sketching and drawing mostly abstract images. It allows me to express myself when I don't have the words.

As for music, we all have those songs that cheer us up or cheer us on. One of those songs for me is "Hear My Song" from the little-known musical review *Songs for a New World*, written by Jason Robert Brown. The song is a passionate plea to hold on and remember that the fight is not yet over. It is an acknowledgment of struggle and a reminder to take a deep breath and know that someone else is in your corner.

While the song opens with a mother speaking to her child, I've often felt it is simply a mentor or friend speaking to someone in need of compassion. I have blared this song in my car with tears leaking from my eyes many times, and somehow it has always made me feel better. It never fails to bring to mind all those people who have had my back and believed me. On the occasions when I have felt utterly desolate and alone, it has reminded me that there are people out there fighting just like me, even if I don't know who they are.

One last question. You call this is a letter you've never sent. Do you think you might send it now? Or find another way to show it to your mom?
To be honest, I don't know. I hope one day I will share it with her, but I know that right now is not the right time. I think, most likely, I will find a way to share the contents with her, but not share the actual letter. I'm not sure when that will be, but I hope it does happen at some point.

SHANYN TODAY

Shanyn Kay Sprague is proud to be a contributor to this anthology. This is her first professional publication.

Shanyn has a heart for those who are struggling to find themselves and those who have been exposed to sexual violence. Currently, she volunteers with a local nonprofit that works with individuals who have experienced sexual assault and/or domestic violence.

While many of her younger years were spent being involved in theater, Shanyn found inspiration and healing in other forms of art as she grew older, including writing, drawing, and baking. Through this variety of art forms, she continues to find new ways to speak her truth. She hopes to encourage others to do the same.

In addition to creating art, Shanyn is an avid reader who enjoys spending time with her friends, visiting museums, finding amazing coffee and music, and quoting TV shows.

DOLL HOUSE

By MISHA KAMAU JAMES TYLER

From above, around the ballfield, the world appeared normal. The sounds of requisite, random gunshots, sirens, crickets, chickens, and traffic occasionally moving up and down Donkey Hill intertwined. There Frank found himself: far from "home," in the apartment that was never really clean, just different versions of disorganized—a disorganization that allowed the roaches to hide in unpredictable ways until they took flight, revealing themselves in a desperate attempt to evade capture. Or reach whatever they perceived as "out": out of the house, out of a window, out of danger, out of sight. More often than not, losing their lives in a nervous-system-driven attempt to preserve their lives.

Two mannequins stood fully dressed in the dining room in Coach couture that changed with the season: this summer, last summer, and next summer. Versace Medusa D'Or dinner plates sat on the table. At all times there was a formal table setting: service plates, butter plates, dinner forks, salad forks, soup spoons, white wine glasses, champagne glasses, red wine glasses, and cloth napkins, in a classic pyramid fold, that matched the gold-and-white linen tablecloth. The tablecloth wrapped itself around a glass table that, when exposed without its vestments, appeared plain, common, and flawed.

No one ate there or sat there. It was as if the table was waiting for the opportunity to meet the right people or have a formal introduction to the idea of food and dining. It was frozen in time, slowing down the progression from the living room to the refrigerator. Really slowing down the access to the freezer, where ice cubes lived that fell in glasses—first in Frank's and then in Magnolia's—bouncing off the bottom of Waterford crystal, soaking in rum or scotch, depending on the mood of the day, the temperature, or the amount of rain that might fall during any given twenty-four hours.

Magnolia in wrap skirts, at the beach, in swimsuits. Magnolia in a thong. Magnolia in high heels. In evening wear. And the famous photo of Magnolia running for Mr. Universe back in the eighties, smiling the same smile of modernity for all time. Always looking intently into the infinity of the camera's lens. Magnolia, always intoxicated by the idea that one day someone might see one of these images—these pictures, these photos disguised as portraits plastered on the walls around the room, on the shelves, on the tables—and that someone might be forced into casual conversation about one of the images. They might comment or praise him. Ask questions regarding their origin. The photos did not adorn him nor did the frames adorn the photos. The images were the idea of happiness frozen in the minutia of time, and if you were lucky, he would offer you a signed copy of your very own.

The fridge was almost empty except for a box of Arm & Hammer baking soda, one package of Boca burgers (for the unforeseen and unlikely future where Magnolia ate healthy), and leftover meals from Blackbeard's Castle that no one would eat. Meals that, no matter how famished, Frank would not allow his hunger or his imagination to fathom the possibility of being edible. These were the leftover parts of lavish dinners out that two bottles of white zinfandel and a bottle of Hennessey would not allow you to finish.

In the living room, there was a cream-colored love seat and an off-white, faded, cracked leather wingback chair, a glass table, metal bookshelves. The shelves held more pictures, photo albums, all the copies of *Vogue, Elle,* and *Glamour* for the year, and pre-internet, glossy, full-color, cheap porn. The latter featured black male models exclusively; arms extended like wings, shorebirds attempting to fly after the BP oil spill, covered in crude—shiny and dying—with an odd beauty. Repetitive, stock images that captured the exact emotional moment in time that Frank and Magnolia could never escape.

Magnolia would tell Frank that he could be in these magazines—any one, all of them.

"You could be one of them, *baby boy,*" he would slowly say in a slightly nasal, drug-induced tone. The floor was dusty, and the broom and mop only seemed to move if someone spilled a drink, and then they only moved to that spot. Frank responded to the pseudo-compliment with silence and contemplation.

The cushions Frank sat on sank in just enough that he had to balance on the couch's edge to look attentive when talking to other people; if he leaned back, he could appear more relaxed than he should at eight in the morning. Frank sat there as the Caribbean sun blazed away, scalding any memory of the last six months—of fall, of the winter he would miss, of his girlfriend MaryAnn. She would tell her friends that Frank left her to move in with a man in the Virgin Islands, encouraging questions about his sexuality to become common conversation, *again*. Frank sat there as the sun scorched away thoughts of his family, of the bars back home, of drinking. The sun scalded away ideas of being drunk, of tears, of crying over pain hidden in dark safe places, the original pain that Magnolia reminded him of; the elderly neighbor's damp, dark basement where Frank initially lost control of his body. This man, who'd paid him in cash as a young teen and enjoyed all the pleasures of Frank's youth. The pains of Christmases past, both real and chimerical, and of the end of the world, which loomed in his mind. Of fear that had taken over in that year, the year that the millennium approached and passed.

He wondered if maybe, as skin became darker, the life he had fled would also change and evolve, perhaps cease to exist.

But despite these haunting memories, Frank looked forward to the daytime. To the sun, to the heat of the morning and afternoon. For he was alone to roam, sober. He felt safe but lost in the warm winter Caribbean sun as he wandered down Main Street, down Back Street, around town, eventually ending up on the beach; Brewer's Bay, Lindbergh Bay, Frenchman's Bay. He was reminded by the ocean that he was on an island, and that there was no further point than "around" that he might venture on any given day. He had evaded winter that year in the Midwest. It had been only a half-dozen months since he had been gone, but so much felt different. He was alone, not in school yet, broke, and somewhat homeless, but not according to Magnolia, who loved the fact that his baby was back home.

Nighttime, alternatively, was the worst. Frank would try to fall asleep in the hot, hard chair—against a wall if he could—upright, drinking himself into a safe stupor, his head to the side. There was only one bedroom in the house, and Cortéz (another wanderer) slept on the couch, beneath the naked lamp that had no shade. He had dreams of being a fashion designer, and in the mind of Magnolia, there was no other place on earth that Cortéz should therefore be than where he could be mentored, reared, fostered, and directed in the ways of the newly out and possibly gay.

Somehow, every day, Cortéz would transform little by little. One piercing at a time. He wore tighter and tighter jeans more fashionably on an island that favored—even borderline required—baggy, until he transformed into a new, uncertain, gay young man with a look of fear—and sometimes detest—for Frank.

The bedroom door was closed sometimes, or just left open a crack. On these nights there was no blanket hiding Frank behind the thin walls. Frank knew that he might have to perform. That he might be remanded to the bedroom, to the darkness beside the cheap alarm clock by the bed, flashing its constantly dying/reanimating green message in desperation. Called by Magnolia's soft, whining voice—a voice that moved like a ghost, a verbal apparition. Magnolia's words were an incantation, floating on the breeze with the nightly thunderstorms that eased their way to Puerto Rico's El Yunque rainforest. Charmed demands that danced in the air, lighting the sky in silence. This was a change from the past. Never before had Frank been in Magnolia's bed, lain next to him. Prior to this, their exchanges were uncomfortable in other ways. Magnolia would take pictures of Frank. Frank would pose for Magnolia in tight underwear while drinking, sitting on the couch, sitting on the bed, standing in the living room.

"Do this for me, baby."

Click, advance, click, advance, click, advance, flash went the little, disposable, cheap, plastic yellow-and-black Kodak camera.

Now Frank's clothes would be eased off and the old man's mouth would search Frank to draw his soul from his body and leave him levitating above the bed somewhere in the room where he could not find himself. Magnolia rubbed his smooth-shaven body on Frank; his hands were not that of a woman. They were not that of a younger man. They were old, smooth, aggressive, and lustful. This was the part Frank liked the least: Magnolia would lay on Frank and attempt to brand his desire into the thing he made Frank's body, searching for a feeling of release.

This was not sex.

Frank took no pleasure in these nights. He did not like lying down, but he did enjoy sleeping in a bed.

The bed was better than the chair. The bed gave some comfort. So Frank would hold to the corner, lying against the cool wall, and hope that he would not need to perform again. Some nights it would not stop; some nights, they would meet the sun, as the fan lazily slung its stagnant air around the room with Magnolia trying to erect himself from the fog of alcohol and drugs and predation.

The memories, brought by day, would invade Frank's mind. Slowly this day/night routine became Frank's "now." Yet it was not a "new" now, it was an old succubus, born years ago and thousands of miles away, unleashed by an elderly man with cash in hand when Frank was only sixteen. And so the hungry demon returned again to feed.

MISHA UNFILTERED
SAFE SPACES

Misha, you suggest that you were alienated from your peers in this story. Did you ever tell them what happened, and were they sympathetic to your situation?

My peers were not aware of my sexual assault when it occurred. I was a teen and just getting a sense of my own sexuality at a point in life when most people are unclear about the person they will be or want to be. It did not even occur to me that the abuse was something that I needed to share or that something that was deeply harmful had even occurred. I was terrified by the experience. I filed it away and tried not to think about it until it occurred again. A lot of people that I consider peers now don't know. One of the fallouts of sexual abuse is fear, so I tend to keep a lot to myself, and I am not always comfortable allowing people so close to me in a meaningful way.

Do you feel that you have recovered from this experience?
I don't feel recovered. I am just in the beginning stages of healing. I have just realized that I need to heal. For a long time I was in denial about the fact that I had been sexually abused. For most of my life I carried a lot of self-blame. It took some time before I realized that something had happened to me that was not in my control. So for me, I have a long road ahead. At least now I know that recovery is something that I can achieve.

Who has helped you get to this point?
One of my best friends created a safe space that allowed me to explore my own sexual abuse, which I had suppressed and reframed so I could cope with it at a young age. She also had similar experiences as a child, so I knew that her viewpoint and her opinion were valid and could be trusted. She encouraged me to go to counseling that was specific for sexual abuse, and I even found a group that was specific to men. I think through my process, her support and understanding was key in allowing me to feel safe asking for help and also in believing that I had the right to heal.

Is everything okay now?
Everything is not always okay. I struggle with self-abusive behavior patterns. It takes a lot of work for me to be aware of my own behavior and my choices at this point in my life. I do a lot of work on acknowledging how I am feeling, but I still have moments where I spiral down a bit. The more awareness I have about these moments, the less gripping power they have over my choices and behavior patterns.

MISHA TODAY

Misha Kamau James Tyler was born in St. Paul, Minnesota. Soon after birth he was whisked away to Milwaukee under the auspices of parental dedication to the Socialist agenda. Russian in name only, growing up in Brew City, he quickly learned he was black, a realization subsequently complemented by a growing suspicion he was also (GASP!) poor. A terminal outsider, he soon fled to the US

Virgin Islands, where he was temporarily satisfied dabbling with an identity more rooted in the diaspora. However, his new home conspired against him, and, alone and unchecked, he slipped down the rabbit hole, becoming the World's First Male-Gender-Identified Cat Lady. He was (and is) a man who loved (and loves) to drink, sit in tall trees, and watch the sun set. The call of global citizenry set in, and in true nomadic fashion, he ended up in Cuidad Juarez. Here he fell in love with a people only moderately less brown than he, developed the working theory that he *may* be an alien, and battled an inner war of monolingualism. Once no one could even pretend to understand a word he was saying, silence became his best friend and he began to write. And write he did . . . for what felt like days . . . and nights . . . and nights . . . and days. After months of wide-eyed, closed-mouth immersion, his Rs were finally rrrrrrolling with the homies; he found children (preferably those under five) and the senior citizen set better than any damn Berlitz.

Misha has read at the Richhold Center for the Performing Arts in St. Thomas, Woodland Pattern Books in Milwaukee, Peoples Books in Milwaukee, UWM, and been a featured guest lecturer at Milwaukee Area Technical College. He is also a farmer and competitive pickler.

A WORD
By SUSAN VAUGHT

IN THE BEGINNING

When It started,
I colored on walls.

I tried to make rainbows.

I tried to pretend.

I
Didn't
Say
A
Word

IN THE MIDDLE

I read Emily Dickinson
And tried not to die
And wrote Emily things that rhymed, like this:

Theme Song

There are some who fear the darkness,
But I, I fear the light.
I need the anonymity
Given by the night.

I'd rather glide in silence,
Unseen by all who try,
Just an image quickly vanished,
A funny trick of eye.

A shadow slipping by them,
That's all I want to be,
Safe within my darkness
And invisibility.

A funny little phantom,
Touched by just a few,
Who see and feel and hear and know
And are but phantoms, too.

*****

I still didn't say a word.

IN THE END

After I kicked him down the stairs,
　　After I cut him and threatened his life and saved my own,
　　After I hurt him,
　　　　After I hurt me,

I wrote this:

Confrontation

Feeling the pressure
Under my eyes,
Stumbling, withering,
Reduced
By my knowledge
Of your games.

I say nothing.

You say everything
Too fast.

*****

I told my friends.

NOW

Sometimes
I
Talk
About
It.

STAY ALIVE

Susan, at the end of your poem, you say, "Sometimes I talk about it."
Can you talk about it?
A man my mother married, a man who was supposed to care for me,
to protect me, used me to meet his own sick needs instead and left
me with physical and emotional scars. I know that sounds vague,
and it is. I think each survivor defines their own personal recovery
and their own personal lines. Some need to discuss specifics, some
have to discuss them in order to heal or help others, and others
select paths in between sharing specifics and refusing outright to
discuss any details. I rarely discuss details, even with close friends—
mostly I talk about thoughts, or effects, or progress from these
events. I have talked a few times, with a therapist, with a few trusted
others, about all the specifics. That's how I chose to no longer be a
victim—dump what I had to in order to leave behind the worst of
the mental health effects. Now, I don't talk about him or what he did.
He's not in my life anymore, or even in the world, and those things
he did, they don't deserve any airplay, not a single second in anyone's
mind. Instead, when the past is heavy on my mind or heart, I talk
about me, and what I need, and where I go from here, today, because
I believe—or struggle to believe, sometimes—that I am what's worth
a few seconds in people's minds and hearts.

I'll honor that sentiment. Let's talk about your journey from then. The
poem culminates in a breakthrough moment where you take action and
find your voice. After that, were you able to make your way to recovery,
and what was most helpful to you in that process?
The most helpful thing for my recovery was getting older, coming
of age, and gaining full possession of my own legal rights, to extract
myself permanently from the abusive situation. During the abuse
itself, I relied on books and reading, music, art, and writing. Fantasy
and science fiction quite literally saved my life by showing me—and
letting me live for a time—in faraway places and magical kingdoms.

My assaults were part of a pattern of abuse that went on for
many years. I learned to tell myself stories, to "live in my head"

afterward, to distance myself from the physical and emotional pain. At first I used dolls to act out stories—similar to the fantasies and science fiction I immersed myself in every day. Later, the characters moved into my head, and I would spend hours imagining their adventures. Time alone away from the world, playing music, and telling myself these stories, those were my comforts.

What about music? If you could get lost in one piece of music, what would it be?
Citizen Cope's "Left for Dead." It's short and simple, and it says everything.

"Been left for dead / I know it's in the back of your head / Been left for dead / Sister, you're better than that."
I could listen to it—have listened to it for hours. Days. It is me.

As you grew older and came to terms with what happened, did you report the crime?
No. This was simply not done when I was a child. I wasn't even sure it was a crime, and I was positive nothing would be done, and I'd be left with the abuser, and he would take his revenge. This happened to friends of mine. It happened to grown women I knew.

In discussions of sexual assault, feminists often point out rape culture—a culture in which rape is normalized or even supported and where victims are blamed for the crime. Do you think rape culture affected your life?
I recently learned about "rape culture" online. In retrospect, I would say, *Hell yes.* I was taught all the things I was supposed to do to avoid sexual assault, an endless list of caring for my own safety. I watched society belittle and reject women who engaged in voluntary sexual relationships, and vilify younger women who became pregnant when they were not married. I clearly received the message that if I was sexually assaulted, it was my fault, and the consequences would be mine to bear. This was the primary reason I chose silence—I knew no help would be forthcoming, and for years, I believed I bore responsibility for my abuse. Rape metaphors, rape jokes, the idiotic things politicians and other people in power say about rape and women's roles in rape touch a deep childhood anger in me now.

I want to see this stop. I want it to become men's responsibility *not* to rape, not women's responsibility to prevent it. I want women's sexuality to be their choice, their bodies to be their province and no one else's. I want people with penises to stop attempting to regulate women's sexual organs and reproduction choices. I never want to hear a rape metaphor or joke ever again.

What advice would you give to a teen or kid in the same situation?
Stay alive. Stay alive, grow up, and recover. Once you can leave the situation, you can heal, even become whole again. You can know true friendship and love, and learn to trust, and you can leave behind the ugliness and pain you face every day now. It's possible. It can happen. Stay alive.

SUSAN TODAY

Susan Vaught is the author of *Footer Davis Probably Is Crazy,* which won the 2016 Edgar Award in the Best Juvenile category. Her many books for teens include *Trigger, Insanity, My Big Fat Manifesto,* and *Freaks Like Us*. She works as a neuropsychologist at a state psychiatric facility, specializing in helping people with severe and persistent mental illness, intellectual disability, and traumatic brain injury. She lives on a farm with her wife and son in rural western Kentucky.

FIRST MEMORY
By LINDA D. WATTLEY

I enjoy having dinner with my son, Marcus. It is a time we exhale, laugh, have great conversations, and enjoy a good meal. But one day in particular I will never forget. We had just had a long laugh when he, out of the blue, changed the subject to memories. I remember like it was yesterday. His words shot through me like a bolt of lightning. I was totally caught off guard. He and his wife were sharing their first childhood memory. Marcus's memory was the night he came to my bedroom to say goodnight.

"I remember coming down the hall to your room, and when I came into your room, you were curled up in bed crying so hard you didn't notice I was there, so I turned and walked away."

I said, "Really?"

"Do you remember your first memory, Mom?"

At first I didn't hear him ask me the question because my mind was still digesting that he saw me crying. I thought I had hidden the pain of my husband's death very well. I didn't want my kids to think life was a sad experience, so going to my room was my way of hiding my pain. My kids were already suffering the death of their father at such a young age. They did not need to know Mommy was unhappy.

"What was your first memory, Mom?" he asked again.

Looking him straight in the eyes, I told him he really didn't want to know.

He asked me, "Is it your dad?"

I nodded my head. "Yes, it's my dad."

That one question sent my memory back fifty years.

At the age of four, I remember being removed from my bed and placed in the middle of my parents' bed. I laid there in the dark, still sleeping. All of a sudden, I felt this sharp pain between my legs. I screamed and cried as I felt my pajamas getting wet. I thought I had wet the bed. The next thing I remembered was my father cradling me and wiping the tears from my eyes. That night, unbeknownst to me, he stole my virginity. For me, it was a night my father comforted me until the pain had subsided, and I dozed off back to sleep. After that night, my father continued to take me from my bed to his bed. All I remembered is being held so gently and lovingly and being touched in a way that put me to sleep.

Things changed over the years. My father took up with a woman who became my stepmother. She had three daughters. When my stepmother would leave to go to work, her oldest daughter and I would stay up late at night, while the other siblings went to bed, and play hide-and-seek with my father. We never talked about it; we just did it. She and I would hide, and when my father would find us, separate or together, we would let him touch us any way he wanted to.

There are other memories, too. Not first memories, but continuing memories—like being eight years old. I was a child who always found comfort in being alone. One day, while lying across my bed reading a book, my stepsister, Reva, came over to me and sat down on the end of the bed. I can still hear her voice today.

"I hate you. I wish you all would get out my momma's house! You so big and fat, and you stink!"

"At least I don't pee in the bed!" I yelled back to her as I realized I better put my book down and get away from her before a fight broke out between us again.

"At least I don't have sex with my father. You are so nasty!"

I tried to say something back, but I couldn't think of anything to say because I didn't understand what she was talking about. *Sex? What is that?* She finally left me alone and headed back downstairs to be with the others. I am not sure what she was talking about, but I did know it sounded like something to be ashamed of. It felt worse than being ashamed to be fat.

Thinking things couldn't get any worse, at the age of ten, I found out the hard way just what it was my stepsister was saying to me.

"What is the matter with you?" my stepmother asked after I had missed my second day of school.

"I don't know. I hurt right here," I said as I pointed to my vaginal area. She took my temperature and found it was high, so she took me to the doctor.

The doctor wanted to do a complete physical and that included a pap smear. I had to take off all my clothes and put on this crepe-paper gown with no sleeves. Then I had to lie down and spread my legs open and place my feet into these stirrups. The room was so cold, and I was so embarrassed this stranger was looking at my private parts. That wasn't the worse of it.

Oh my God! He took some cold jelly-like stuff and used his fingers to feel inside my vagina. That was so gross and painful. When he was finished, he told me to get dressed and asked my stepmother to come with him. When she came back, I thought I was in serious trouble because she was very angry, and tears were slowly flowing from her eyes.

"Has anybody ever touched you down there?"

"No, I use tissue to wipe myself after I pee. That's all that happens down there."

"I am going to ask you one more time, and then I am going to whip your ass if you don't tell me the truth. One more time, who touched you down there?"

"The only other thing I can think of is when me, Daddy, and Peggy play hide-and-seek. He plays with it when he catches me and that's it," I said.

"That's it? Wait till we get home, you just wait!" she whispered.

The drive back home was very quiet. My stepmother did not seem to realize I was in the car. She was very angry and seemed to be hurt about something. As we approached our three-level home where all the other children were outside playing, she told everybody to stay outside except Peggy and me. Peggy looked at me and I looked at her as though I had no clue what was going on.

Peggy barely made it into the living room before my stepmother grabbed her and slammed her up against the wall. I felt so sorry for Peggy—her own mother was handling her like she was a stranger trying to rob her.

"What in the hell have you been doing when I leave to go to work at night?" she yelled.

Peggy just fell to the floor. She covered her face with her hands and started crying so hard it made me cry. All three of us was crying, but my stepmother was the only one shouting words that didn't make any sense. When she couldn't get any answers out of Peggy, she threatened to beat the life out of her.

"Nothing, Mommy! Nothing! Just playing a game with Daddy!" she cried.

"You know better, don't you?!" she yelled. "What did your daddy do to you?! Did you have sex with him?"

"No, ma'am! Yes, ma'am!" Peggy cried and tried to run past her to the front door of the house.

She didn't make it before my stepmother snatched her by her hair and knocked her down to the floor. Just when she was going to slap her, my father came in and grabbed her hand and told me and Peggy to go upstairs. We ran upstairs while they fought like cats and dogs.

Things were never the same after that day. Peggy and I were no longer allowed to stay up late while the other kids went to bed. My father and stepmother somehow managed to get past it without telling anybody about it.

Life went on as though it never happened.

When I turned sixteen, I was beginning to learn what it was like to have a boy hug and kiss me. It felt strange at first because a boy was not the first person to do this to me; it was my father. I managed to observe the feelings that came when I was being touched by the boys. Oftentimes, I felt like crying because it did not feel right. There were times I wanted more of it to see if it would make me happy. When I did have moments of actually enjoying it, I felt special.

One day, I had an unforgettable life-changing experience. It was the day I finally stood up for myself.

I was still the little girl who found contentment being alone. One evening I was alone in our basement listening and dancing to music when I felt someone grab me from behind and wrap their arms around me.

"No! Please, stop!" I cried as I realized that person was my father. I cried and screamed so much it frightened him. He looked at me like I had literally broken his heart.

"I will never touch you again. I promise!" My father said as tears appeared in his eyes. He then turned and walked away. I remember feeling so awful he wanted to touch me like boys touch girls; I also felt bad because I could tell his feelings were hurt.

Two hours later, I found out my father was shot in the back and paralyzed from the waist down. My stepmother had shot him in the back as he was walking from the top floor of our house to leave for work. Apparently he had decided to end the relationship, and she was not going to let him go.

My father promised to not touch me again and on that day he never walked again. How ironic is that? He had no more feelings from the waist down. Oftentimes, I felt it was my fault this happened to him. But eventually I realized, more importantly, it was the day I spoke up for myself.

"Mom, are you alright? Looked like you left me for a minute there."

My son filtered back into my view. Here. Now. At the dinner table.

"The first memory . . . it was your dad?"

"Yes, it was my dad."

LINDA UNFILTERED
EMBRACE YOURSELF

Linda, your stepsister taunted you about the abuse in a shaming way. That's generally regarded as "victim blaming." How did it affect how you viewed yourself?
I felt responsible because I allowed it. Something about it made me feel special to him. I wasn't feeling special to anyone else. My relationships were affected by it from the standpoint I could be with anybody no matter how kind or unkind they were. I felt people's happiness was a priority over my own. I didn't see myself as mattering, only providing what people wanted to keep peace and have a relationship.

Did you end up in damaging relationships? Was that a cycle you had to break?
Basically, I felt unworthy of having quality people in my life. My relationship with the opposite sex was always on their terms. I gave my time, money, and body to them because I felt they deserved it just because they wanted me around. They didn't have to prove they wanted or loved me. It wasn't until I met my husband, someone who

actually embraced me just as I was, that I came to realize I could be valued by someone because he made me see myself. He told me he knew something was wrong with me because I always had to be doped up or drinking alcohol to enjoy life. I had no idea I was doing that. His love and patience with me broke the cycle.

In your story, you lack allies. In particular, none of the adults in the situation stopped it. The doctor and your stepmother knew, but things continued. Do you know why?
I am not sure what my stepmother told the doctor, and he was no longer mentioned in my presence. I do know that my stepmother was the main and only adult who knew about the abuse I and my stepsister experienced. She told no one. And we were told to not tell anyone because she didn't want us to suffer public shame if it reached the newspapers. She cursed my father verbally, and they had a horrific fight over it, but she never left him. We had to go on as if it never happened.

Was there a breakthrough moment where you knew you would be okay?
Yes, when I looked at my two sons whom I had raised alone after my husband was suddenly killed in a car accident. I realized how awesome they were! I did extremely well raising and protecting them from potential unnecessary harm. I am proud I was able to pull out the best in myself to make sure they had a normal and healthy life.

What would you like to say to a teen or kid in your situation?
If one person has been able to be happy and live a normal life after being abused, then you, too, can give yourself time to get there. Save yourself from the worst aspects of yourself by embracing the child who had the experience. Protect her or him like you wished you had been protected. Remember, you will always be the first child you will ever have. Embrace yourself knowing you have the power to be more than your feelings are saying you are. One day, your feelings will change and you will be so happy.

LINDA TODAY

Linda Diane Wattley is a published writer who began her first work of art with poetry. The poem "I Wish" appeared in the Poetry Gem of American Poets Society. For over twelve years she had her own religious/philosophical column in the *Frost Illustrated* newspaper entitled "The Best Will Show Themselves." Today, God has awakened her to a new and extremely important message to share with the world. We must become more conscious of PTSD. She is presenting her newest work: *Soldier with a Backpack: Living and Dying Simultaneously.* This work reveals the reality of the impact this disorder has on the lives of our veterans and civilians.

Wattley is also a motivational speaker who looks forward to sharing her life's tools of getting beyond survival to living after experiencing victimization.

HEART

By CAROL LYNCH WILLIAMS

I

MatthewMarkLukeJohn

Matthew, my best friend in first grade.
Watching movies, wrassling, collecting frogs that fell from clouds.

The oldest brother just needed to know.
John said, "You can help me."

In the bushes.
In the horse pasture.
Behind our houses.

The first day it happened the sky was blue enough to hurt.

II

Mom said, later,
years later,
after the stepgrandfather,
"What? Why will they believe you now?
After you let that happen."

She was right.

In court, the jury said they didn't want us to testify again
because it was too hard for such young girls
(my sister three years younger than me).
They let Floyd go free
and with all those other children
at home.

My cousins, too.
My cousins, too.

III

Ross.
The professor at a local university.
(I just looked up his picture online.
That's him!
He never married!
He's dead!)

"You don't remember?" my sister asked. "I was in second grade."
(We both had children, when she spoke of him.
Her face flat in the telling.
No emotion.
Just the facts.)

I saw him in the shadow of memory.
"No. Nothing."
"Nothing? Well. I remember it all."
I shrugged.
"And you were there," she said.

Memory shows me in the closet, waiting.
Waiting.

IV

All these years later, I call my daughters aside, one at a time.
"I'm writing this," I say. "Will you be embarrassed to know what
happened to me?"
"Never! No!"

But I'm overcome with shame.
I am.
Logic says it wasn't my fault.
Not my doing.

Still
reading these words over,
I blanch.

Want to hide.
Not sign my name.

Does even one of them,
one of those men,
feel even a little like I do?

Or are they free,
each one, with *his* memories?

V

I never want a child to feel this way.
Never want a girl or boy to carry
the feelings I have
for so long.

And so I write.

Because maybe,
maybe, maybe
someone will find this—
read these words
and not be shamed
not be afraid.
Have the heart
to speak
out.

CAROL UNFILTERED
JUSTICE WAS SERVED

Carol, your poem ends with finding the courage to speak out. Let's start with the first time you found your voice. Who was the first person you confided in?

The story is really complex. I think many times when a person is abused it happens more than once, and that was the case with me. The first incident was with MatthewMarkLukeJohn, you know—the next-door neighbor. And I never told anyone about that.

A few years later, however, I went to my aunt's house. I was going to stay for several weeks and just have fun playing with my cousins. The abuser in this case was an elderly man—the stepgrandfather to my cousin.

After the incident, I spoke first to my aunt through a note. I told her what happened. It turned out the man was a serial pedophile and had been abusing all the children in his family.

My aunt called Mom, who drove the several hours to pick me up. While she was coming to get us, my aunt and the abuser's wife and sister got me in the car. We drove into the sticks. I remember there were no houses. We were just on a dirt road driving to nowhere. The women in the car kept saying things like, "If you tell, he'll go to jail." "If you tell, the police will kill him. Do you want him killed?" "Please, don't do it. Do you want him to die?"

I remember looking out the window and thinking, yes, I *did* want him to die.

My aunt sat silent. Perhaps she thought I was lying. She considered her daughter a liar—and my cousin had also been abused.

When this whole thing blew up in court, my aunt wouldn't allow her daughter to testify because she said her child was a liar, even though this child could explain what an erect adult penis looked like. The thought makes me sick.

What in the world were these adults thinking? It just blows my mind. And that my aunt wouldn't listen to her daughter? I'm sure that what was going on for my poor, younger cousin was far worse than what happened to me.

That is terrible. Can you tell us what court was like?
Litigation was awful. We were so young. I think I was nine, maybe eight, but maybe not. All my memories seem focused to only one or two ages. We had to tell, in detail, what had happened to us. It was embarrassing.

To make matters worse, it was at this point that I revealed to my mother that it happened with our next-door neighbor many years earlier. She was sort of disgusted with me. "They'll never believe you," she said. And she was sort of right.

Was justice ever served? Where is he now?
They let him go. The court felt it was too traumatic to make us go through a jury trial, so they let that pedophile free to abuse again.

However, I would like to think that justice was served. This man is dead. I actually do believe in God, and I believe in a God whose Son said, "But whoso shall offend one of these little ones which believe in me, it were better for him that a millstone were hanged about his neck, and that he were drowned in the depth of the sea"—Matthew 18:6.

All these years later I'm sorta hoping for the worst for him.

You've left the past behind, grown, written stories, had children of your own. You're successful by so many standards. Is everything okay now?
I'm not sure if everything is okay. I mean, I think I'm okay, but I'm really old now. What my experience did for me was make me a mother who was really aware of what was going on with her children. Especially when my girls were young. Also sort of a fighter for others. I look when a baby cries. I watch parents with their children in the grocery store. I offer help for mothers who seem frustrated and tired.

What's helped you the most to recover and heal?
I never really went for help in any of the incidents that occurred. In fact, when you use the word *crime* in some of your questions, I sort of wonder if I am worthy to say that a crime was committed against me. A crime every time? Yes. A crime *every* time.

What I have done for myself, though, is write. I write about the hard stuff. I write about sexual abuse. I write about mothers who betray their daughters. Write about pain and sorrow. I think writing is a healing process.

CAROL TODAY

Carol Lynch Williams, who grew up in Florida and now lives in Utah, is an award-winning novelist with seven children of her own, including six daughters. She has an MFA in writing for children and young adults from Vermont College, and she won the prestigious PEN/Phyllis Naylor Working Writer Fellowship. *The Chosen One* (2009) was named one of the ALA's Quick Picks for Reluctant Young Adult Readers and Best Books for Young Adult Readers. It won the Whitney and the Association of Mormon Letters awards for the best young adult novel of the year. It was featured on numerous lists of recommended YA fiction. Carol's other novels include *Glimpse; Miles from Ordinary; The Haven; Waiting; Signed, Skye Harper; Never Said;* and *Messenger.*

WHERE TO FIND HELP

If you are in immediate danger, call 911

Sexual violence is never ok. As you've read in the brave stories these survivors have shared, abuse plays out in many forms and victims and survivors are often shamed into silence. It's important to remember that verbal, emotional and mental abuse are still abuse.

If you feel that you have been violated, call the numbers below. If you're confused and trying to figure out if a situation was abusive and need to talk it out, call the numbers below. If you found a story in the book that mirrors your own life or an experience you had, call the numbers below. You are not alone. There is help out there.

National Sexual Assault Hotline (RAINN): 800-656-4673 (HOPE)

Darkness to Light: 1-866-367-5444 (FOR-LIGHT)

National Human Trafficking Hotline: 1-888-373-7888

Love Is Respect.org Helpline: 1-866-331-9474

Stop It Now! Helpline: 1-888-773-8368 (PREVENT)

For a listing of regional crisis centers, visit http://centers.rainn.org.

STATISTICS

Quantifying sexual violence in our society today is difficult. Statistics related to sexual violence can be hard to gather and evaluate, and different studies and statistics can't always be directly compared. While numerous studies have been conducted, and these help us define the scope or extent of sexual violence, much remains to be learned. In other words, what I provide here is not exhaustive or definitive, but it reflects a brief summary of what we know. New studies and surveys are conducted regularly, so what I provide here will likely change.

The reason that sexual violence is hard to get a bead on is inherent in the issue of sexual violence itself. As this book testifies, society does not like to discuss sexual violence, which discourages people from speaking out. Incidents often go unreported or are underreported, which masks the true extent of the problem. One 2015 report said that only about a third of rape and sexual assaults are reported to the police (Truman and Morgan). Think about that: Perhaps two-thirds of sexual assaults go unreported. Many of the reasons why victims don't report these crimes have already been discussed by this book's contributors, and studies confirm what they say: Victims fear reprisal (or being shamed), they consider it a personal matter (one that involves their immediate family), or they think the police can't or won't help (Planty).

Then, when episodes of sexual violence are reported, they may not always be understood in the same way, even by the people involved. As we've seen, especially with children, the ability to articulate and understand what happened varies greatly depending on the victim's age, the awareness and help of others, the resources available, and the ability or willingness to speak to police, advocates, and so on. Further, each state has different legal definitions related to sexual violence, so even official statistics can be hard to compare. I've provided a list of the works I cite at the the back of the book, but I urge you to seek out current or updated information online. A good place to start are recent publications from the Department of Justice.

For our purposes here, I've gathered information that helps answer three main questions: Who are the victims? Who are the perpetrators? And what are the health effects of victimization?

Who Are the Victims?

Statistics differ between children and adults. For victims under age eighteen, the Children's Bureau of the US Department of Health and Human Services substantiated or found strong evidence that 57,286 children were victims of sexual abuse in 2015 alone (*Child Maltreatment 2015*). While that's a daunting number, it only reflects reported cases nationwide, so it doesn't reflect or account for unreported cases. As a percentage or ratio, one 2014 study indicated that 1 in 9 girls and 1 in 53 boys will experience sexual abuse at the hands of an adult by age eighteen. However, more broadly, the same study said that 1 in 4 girls and 1 in 20 boys will experience sexual abuse *or* assault by any age perpetrator by age eighteen (Finkelhor).

For victims over the age of eighteen, the Department of Justice reports that females between the ages of eighteen and twenty-four are more likely to experience rape or sexual assault than any other age group (Sinozich). The rate of rape and sexual assault differs somewhat with student and nonstudent status. In a 2014 report, the rate for female nonstudents was 7.6 per 1,000 women, and for female students it was 6.1 per 1,000 (Sinozich). Male students, on the other hand, were at an increased risk compared to nonstudents. The rate for male nonstudents was 0.3 per 1,000, while for male students it was 1.4 per 1,000 (Langton).

In general, as a society, we have been talking more about sexual violence on college campuses than ever before. A good report on campus sexual violence is *Report on the AAU Campus Climate Survey on Sexual Assault and Sexual Misconduct* by David Cantor. One detail I found particularly upsetting in this report was that 16.5 percent of college seniors reported experiencing sexual contact (such as sexual touching or penetration) as a result of physical force or incapacitation. This report breaks down rates of sexual violence among all students by gender: 26.1 percent of female students experienced sexual violence, and 6.3 percent of males. However, transgender, genderqueer, and gendernonconforming (TGCN) students experienced the highest rate of victimization at 29.5 percent.

A 2004 US Department of Justice report (Perry) distinguished the rates of violent crime (which includes sexual violence) by race. Among people age twelve and older, American Indians suffered the highest rate of 5 victimizations per 1,000 people. Next, white and black Americans had a rate of 2 per 1,000 and Asian Americans were 1 per 1,000.

Who Are the Perpetrators?

Multiple studies indicate that the majority of sexual abuse perpetrators are known to their victims, whether the victims are children or adults. In 2015, the federal Children's Bureau reported that in child sexual abuse cases, 78.1 percent of perpetrators were a parent of their victim, 6.3 percent were a relative other than a parent, and 4.1 percent had a relationship to either multiple victims in the same report or multiple victims across reports. Also, 3.7 percent of perpetrators were an unmarried partner to the victim's parent (*Child Maltreatment 2015*).

As we've seen, not all perpetrators are adults. Another study indicated that the lifetime rate of sexual abuse and assault for seventeen-year-old females by juvenile perpetrators was 17.8 percent; for seventeen-year-old males, it was 3.1 percent. This same study said that, regardless of age, perpetrators were only rarely strangers. Perpetrators who were unknown to the victim only 3 percent among females and 1.4 among males (Finkelhor).

Among women, the trend of known perpetrators continues into adulthood. One study found that among all women, 78 percent of sexual violence involved an offender who was a family member, intimate partner, friend, or acquaintance (Planty). Meanwhile, a separate study of college-age women (whether victims were students or not) found that 80 percent of women knew their offender (Sinozich and Langton). One exception to this trend is in Native American/Native Alaskan communities, where 41 percent of sexual assaults are committed by a stranger (Perry).

As for the perceived race of perpetrators, one study of female victims found that perpetrators were 57 percent white, 27 percent black, 6 percent other, 1 percent mixed, and 8 percent unknown (Planty).

How Does Victimization Affect Health?

Of course, victims of sexual violence experience a multitude of health issues. Many studies have indicated elevated physical health risks, including gastrointestinal problems, muscle and joint pain, cardiopulmonary symptoms, and gynecological pain (Irish). Pregnancy and sexually transmitted diseases are also issues, but these are harder to quantify accurately, since it can be difficult to confirm preexisting versus incident-related conditions. For a general analysis, see RAINN's "Victims of Sexual Violence: Statistics" (https://www.rainn.org/statistics/victims-sexual-violence).

Mental health issues are easier to identify through self-reporting surveys. A 2014 US Department of Justice report indicated that 75 percent of rape and sexual assault victims experience socio-emotional problems (Langton and Truman). This includes struggling with distress, anxiety, and relationships with peers, family members, and coworkers. In the aftermath of violence, 38 percent of victims indicated problems at work and school, and 27 percent indicated family and friend relationship problems. When it came to stress, 46 percent reported severe distress, 26 percent reported moderate distress, and 18 percent reported mild distress, while only 11 percent reported no distress at all. Another study in 2005 indicated that children who were sexually abused are two times more likely than unabused peers to attempt suicide later in life. Child victims also showed increased risk as adults of having alcohol problems, using illicit drugs, and having depression (Shanta).

In the end, what all these numbers mean is that we have a large societal issue to contend with when it comes to sexual violence. However, there are positive signs. One report noted that from 1995 to 2010, the total rate of rape and sexual assaults against females (age twelve and older) declined by 58 percent (Planty). If reliable, that would be significant progress, but much work still needs to be done. The more we listen, empathize, strategize, articulate, report sexual violence, and utilize victim services, the more barriers collapse and perceptions change. When we do this, we come closer to minimizing risk and maximizing potential for a better society. One way we do that is by speaking out and telling stories.

WORDS AND TERMS

The language around sexual violence is an ongoing and evolving conversation. Legal definitions of words like *consent, assault, incest,* and *rape* vary from state to state—so what constitutes consent in New Hampshire does not constitute consent in Alabama. I've noted below which terms can vary by state, and you can find some of these state-by-state legal definitions by visiting RAINN's "State Law Database" (https://apps.rainn.org/policy).

The definitions below reflect much of what you've seen in the book and are derived from multiple sources. Most are official or legal definitions as provided by federal agencies and the American Psychiatric Association. These sources are indicated at the end of a definition by an abbreviation, such as "CDC" (for Centers of Disease Control), and the sources themselves are listed at the end of this book. Terms without a source are my own phrasing, sometimes based on a standard dictionary.

Alternative therapies: Any of a range of medical therapies that are not regarded as orthodox by the medical profession, such as herbalism, homeopathy, and acupuncture.

Anorexia: Eating disorder featuring persistent energy intake restriction, intense fear of gaining weight or of becoming fat, or persistent behavior that interferes with weight gain and a disturbance in personal perception of weight or shape (DSM-5).

Bipolar disorder: A mood disorder featuring swings in mood from manic highs to depressive episodes. Generally, mild symptoms indicate Bipolar I, while severe swings and a major depressive episode indicate Bipolar II (DSM-5).

Borderline personality disorder: A personality disorder featuring patterns of instability of interpersonal relationships, self-image, and affects, and marked impulsivity that begins by early adulthood (DSM-5).

Child sexual abuse: The employment, use, persuasion, inducement, enticement, or coercion of any child to engage in, or assist any other person to engage in, any sexually explicit conduct or simulation of such conduct for the purpose of producing a visual depiction of such conduct. Or the rape, and in case of caretaker or inter-familial relationships, statutory rape, molestation, prostitution, or other form of sexual exploitation of children, or incest with child (CAPTA).

Consent: Words or overt actions by a person who is legally or functionally competent to give informed approval, indicating a freely given agreement to have sexual intercourse or sexual contact (CDC). Consult your state's legal definition.

Depression: Depressive disorder featuring the presence of sad, empty, or irritable moods that significantly affect functioning (DSM-5).

Inability to consent: A freely given agreement to have sexual contact could not occur because of the victim's age, illness, mental or physical disability, being asleep or unconscious, or being too intoxicated (e.g. incapacitation, lack of consciousness, or lack of awareness) through their voluntary or involuntary use of alcohol or drugs (CDC).

Inability to refuse: Disagreement to engage in a sexual act was precluded because of the use or possession of guns or other nonbody weapons, or due to physical violence, threats of physical violence, intimidation or pressure, or misuse of authority (CDC).

Incest: Sexual intercourse between persons so closely related that they are forbidden by law to marry. Consult your state's legal definition.

Incident: A single act or series of acts of sexual violence that are perceived to be connected to one another and that may persist over a period of minutes, hours, or days. One perpetrator or multiple perpetrators may commit an incident (CDC).

Perpetrator: Person who inflicts sexual violence (CDC).

PTSD (posttraumatic stress disorder): A trauma- and stressor-related disorder that occurs from experiencing or witnessing a traumatic event. Symptoms of PTSD include recurrent intrusive memories of the event, recurrent distressing dreams of the event, dissociative reactions in which the individual feels like the traumatic event is recurring, intense psychological distress at internal or external cues that resemble the stressor, memory lapses, and avoidance (DSM-5).

Rape: Forced sexual intercourse including both psychological coercion as well as physical force. Forced sexual intercourse means vaginal, anal, or oral penetration by the offender(s). This category also includes incidents where the penetration is from a foreign object such as a bottle. Includes attempted rapes, male as well as female victims, and both heterosexual and same-sex rape. Attempted rape includes verbal threats of rape (BJS). Note that definitions of rape vary widely, and legally it's sometimes called "aggravated felonious sexual assault" or "gross sexual assault," among others. Consult your state's legal definition.

Rape culture: A culture in which is rape is normalized, trivialized, or condoned. Victims are charged with being responsible for their own safety, and the subject is largely stigmatized. Rape culture is perpetuated by victim-blaming language, stigma, and glorification of aggression.

Rape kit: Also known as "physical evidence collection." The collection of hairs, fibers, or specimens of body fluids from a victim's body or garments that may aid in identification of the perpetrator (CDC).

Rape myth: Pervasive misconceptions about how rape plays out and how victims respond. Common myths include the following statements: Rape only happens as a violent crime by a stranger; rape victims commonly lie about being raped; men and boys are not victims of sexual violence; if a person wears the right clothes, they can avoid being raped; and if the victim does not fight back, they wanted it.

Sexual assault: A wide range of victimizations, separate from rape or attempted rape. These crimes include attacks or attempted attacks generally involving unwanted sexual contact between victim and offender. Sexual assaults may or may not involve force and include such things as grabbing or fondling. Sexual assault also includes verbal threats (BJS). Consult your state's legal definition.

Sexual trafficking: The recruitment, harboring, transportation, provision, or obtaining of a person for the purpose of commercial sex act. In order for a situation to be considered trafficking, it must have at least one of the elements within each of the three criteria of process, means, and goal. If one condition from each criterion is met, the result is trafficking. For adults, victim consent is irrelevant if one of the means is employed. For children, consent is irrelevant with or without the means category. (Process: recruitment, transportation, transferring, harboring, or receiving. Means: threat coercion, abduction, fraud, deceit, deception, or abuse of power. Goal: prostitution, pornography, violence/sexual exploitation, or involuntary sexual servitude.) (CDC)

Sexual violence: A sexual act that is committed or attempted by another person without freely given consent of the victim or against someone who is unable to consent or refuse (due to victim's age, illness, mental or physical disability, being asleep or unconscious, or being too intoxicated). It includes forced or alcohol/drug facilitated penetration of a victim; forced or alcohol/drug facilitated incidents in which the victim was made to penetrate a perpetrator or someone else; nonphysically pressured unwanted penetration. Intentional sexual touching; or noncontact acts of a sexual nature. Sexual violence can also occur when a perpetrator forces or coerces a victim to engage in sexual acts with a third party (CDC).

Statutory Rape: Sexual relations with a minor. Consult your state's legal definition.

Substance use disorder: A substance-related disorder featuring cluster of cognitive, behavioral, and physiological symptoms indicating that the individual continues using the substance despite substance-related problems. Basically, a pathological use of a substance despite related negative effects (DSM-5).

Survivor: Often synonymous with *victim* (see below); a person who survives an incident of sexual violence.

Victim: Person on whom the sexual violence is inflicted (CDC).

Victim advocate: Services provided by someone trained in violent crime response that usually occur by phone, in person, or in a hospital setting. The services may include crisis response, information, support, and referral (CDC).

Victim blaming: When someone blames the victim instead of the perpetrator of an act of sexual violence, or casting doubt on a victim's account, often by asserting that the victim was responsible for the harm that occurred.

ONLINE RESOURCES
ORGANIZATIONS AND ADVOCACY GROUPS

1in6 (https://1in6.org): An organization that helps men who have survived sexual violence in childhood.

Darkness to Light (www.darknesstolight.org): An organization working to end child sexual abuse. Runs a hotline.

Girlthrive (www.girlthrive.org): An organization specifically honoring teen girls of child sexual abuse through scholarships, opportunity, and education.

Joyful Heart Foundation (www.joyfulheartfoundation.org): Resources to heal, educate, and empower survivors of sexual assault, domestic violence, and child abuse.

Learning Hope (www.learninghope.org): An online resource for childhood sexual abuse survivors. It includes information on myths and facts, storywalls, and a blog.

Love Is Respect.org (www.loveisrespect.org): Resources and information on healthy relationships. Empowerment initiative for young people to prevent and end dating violence. Can chat or text online, or call their helpline.

Male Survivor (www.malesurvivor.org): Resources, forums, reporting information, and advocacy specific to male survivors of sexual violence.

Men Can Stop Rape (www.mencanstoprape.org): An organization dedicated to mobilizing men to use their strength for creating cultures free from violence, especially gender-based violence.

National Sex Offender Public Website (NSOPW, www.nsopw.gov): Run by the US Department of Justice, this office handles sex offender sentencing, monitoring, apprehending, registering, and tracking.

Rape and Incest National Network (RAINN, www.rainn.org): The largest national resource for victims of sexual violence. Find statistics, information on reporting, local rape crisis centers, survival stories, speakers bureaus, ways to get involved, and a hotline.

Stop It Now! (http://www.stopitnow.org): Resources for teachers and allies to help prevent child sexual abuse, including trainings and prevention measures. For survivors, email or chat online, or call the hotline.

Survivors of Incest Anonymous (www.siawso.org): A recovery resource and community for survivors of incest.

The Unslut Project (www.unslutproject.com): An organization that focuses on putting an end to sexual bullying; connected to the 2016 documentary film *Unslut*.

Voices and Faces Project (www.voicesandfaces.org): A documentary initiative focused on bringing survivor stories to public attention to make change. Voices and Faces is a place to hear survivor stories, speak out, learn about advocacy, and become part of the movement to end sexual violence.

RECOMMENDED READING

Recommended Nonfiction Titles
This list of nonfiction titles includes personal accounts on sexual violence, books that can help the healing process, books that envision a world without rape, and investigations of rape and assault in our society and on college campuses.

Dick, Kirby, and Amy Ziering. *The Hunting Ground: The Inside Story of Sexual Assault on American College Campuses.* New York: Hot Books, 2015.

Friedman, Jaclyn, and Jessica Valenti. *Yes Means Yes!: Visions of Female Sexual Power and a World Without Rape.* Berkeley, CA: Seal Press, 2008.

Gay, Roxane. *Bad Feminist.* New York: Harper Perennial, 2014.

Harding, Kate. *Asking for It: The Alarming Rise of Rape Culture—and What We Can Do about It.* Boston: Da Capo Lifelong Books, 2015.

Herman, Judith L. *Trauma and Recovery: The Aftermath of Violence—From Domestic Abuse to Political Terror.* New York: Basic Books, 2015

Krakauer, Jon. *Missoula: Rape and the Justice System in a College Town.* New York: Doubleday, 2015.

Lehman, Carolyn. *Strong At the Heart: How It Feels to Heal from Sexual Abuse.* New York: Farrar, Straus, and Giroux, 2005.

Lindin, Emily. *Unslut: A Diary and a Memoir.* San Francisco: Zest Books, 2015.

Patterson, Jennifer. *Queering Sexual Violence: Radical Voices from Within the Anti-Violence Movement.* Riverdale, NY: Riverdale Avenue Books, 2016.

Prout, Chessy, with Jenn Abelson. *I Have the Right To: A High School Survivor's Story of Sexual Assault, Justice, and Hope.* New York: Margaret K. McElderry Books, 2018.

Raja, Sheela, and Jaya Ashrafi. *The PTSD Survival Guide for Teens: Strategies to Overcome Trauma, Build Resilience, and Take Back Your Life.* Oakland, CA: Instant Help, 2018.

Ream, Anne K. *Lived Through This: Listening to the Stories of Sexual Violence Survivors.* Boston: Beacon Press, 2014.

Sher, Abby. *Breaking Free: True Stories of Girls Who Escaped Modern Slavery.* Hauppauge, NY: Barron's Educational Series, 2014.

van der Kolk, Bessel A. *The Body Keeps the Score: Brain, Mind, and Body in the Healing of Trauma.* New York: Viking, 2014.

Stoin, Maria. *Take It as a Compliment.* London: Singing Dragon, 2015.

Una. *Becoming Unbecoming.* Brighton, England: Myriad Editions, 2015.

Wattley, Linda Diane. *Soldier with a Backpack: Living and Dying Simultaneously.* North Plainfield, NJ: After the Storm Publishing, 2015.

Recommended Fiction Titles

This list of young adult fiction includes titles that tackle rape, sexual assault, sexual abuse, and incest from a variety of perspectives.

Anderson, Laurie. *Speak.* New York: Macmillan, 1999.

Blount, Patty. *Some Boys.* Naperville, IL: Sourcebooks Fire, 2014.

Chbosky, Stephen. *Perks of Being A Wallflower.* New York: Simon and Schuster, 1999.

Cribbs, G. Donald. *The Packing House.* Booktrope Editions, 2016.

Desir, Christa. *Fault Line.* New York: SimonPulse, 2013.

Frank, E.R. *Dime.* New York: Atheneum, 2015.

Goobie, Beth. *The Pain Eater.* Toronto, Canada: Second Story Press, 2017.

Hallbrook, Kristin. *Every Last Promise.* New York: HarperTeen, 2015.

Hartzler, Aaron. *What We Saw.* New York: HarperTeen, 2015

Hopkins, Ellen. *Identical.* New York: Margaret K. McElderry Books, 2008.

Johnston, E.K. *Exit, Pursued by a Bear.* New York: Dutton Books for Young Readers, 2007.

Knowles, Jo. *Lessons from a Dead Girl.* Somerville, MA: Candlewick, 2007.

Krossing, Karen. *Punch Like a Girl.* Custer, WA: Orca Book Publishers, 2015.

Leavitt, Martine. *My Book of Life, By Angel.* New York: Farrar, Straus, and Giroux, 2012.

Levine, Ellen. *In Trouble.* Minneapolis: Carolrhoda Lab, 2011.

Lynch, Chris. *Inexcusable.* New York: Atheneum Books for Young

Readers, 2007.

McCormick, Patricia. *Sold.* New York: Hyperion, 2006.

Melanie, Florence. *One Night.* Toronto, Canada: James Lorimer and
    Company, 2016.

O'Neill, Louise. *Asking for It.* New York: Quercus, 2015.

Padian, Maria. *Wrecked.* New York: Algonquin Young Readers, 2016.

Sapphire. *Push.* New York: Vintage, 1997.

Shaw, Susan. *Safe.* New York: Dutton Childrens Books, 2007.

Smith, Amber. *The Way I Used to Be.* New York: Margaret K.
    McElderry Books, 2016.

Stevens, Courtney C. *Faking Normal.* New York: HarperTeen, 2014.

Summers, Courtney. *All The Rage.* New York: St. Martin's Griffin, 2015.

Williams-Garcia, Rita. *Every Time a Rainbow Dies.* New York:
    Amistad, 2001.

Works Cited: Statistics

Cantor, David, et al. "Report on the AAU Campus Climate Survey on Sexual
Assault and Sexual Misconduct." Association of American Universities
(September 21, 2015): xiii, www.aau.edu/sites/default/files/@%20Files/
Climate%20Survey/AAU_Campus_Climate_Survey_12_14_15.pdf.

Child Maltreatment 2015. Children's Bureau, US Department of Health
    and Human Services, Administration for Children and Families,
    Administration on Children Youth and Families (2017): 45, 55, 66, www.acf.
    hhs.gov/sites/default/files/cb/cm2015.pdf.

Finkelhor, David, et al. "The Lifetime Prevalence of Child Sexual Abuse and
    Sexual Assault Assessed in Late Adolescence." *Journal of Adolescent Health*
    (July 2014): 329–33, www.unh.edu/ccrc/pdf/9248.pdf.

Irish, Leah, et al. "Long-Term Physical Health Consequences of Childhood
    Sexual Abuse: A Meta-Analytic Review." *Journal of Pediatric Psychology* 35,
    no. 5 (December 2009): 450–61, www.ncbi.nlm.nih.gov/pubmed/20022919.

Langton, Lynn, and Jennifer Truman. "Socio-emotional Impact of Violent
    Crime." US Department of Justice, Bureau of Justice Statistics, Office of
    Justice Programs (September 2014): 1, 5, 17, www.bjs.gov/content/pub/pdf/
    sivc.pdf.

Perry, Stephen W. "American Indians and Crime." US Department of Justice,
    Bureau of Justice Statistics, Office of Justice Programs (December 2004): 8,
    www.bjs.gov/content/pub/pdf/aic02.pdf.

Planty, Michael, et al. "Female Victims of Sexual Violence, 1994–2010." US
    Department of Justice, Bureau of Statistics, Office of Justice Programs
    (March 2013): 1, 5, 7, www.bjs.gov/content/pub/pdf/fvsv9410.pdf.

Shanta, R. Dube, et al. "Long-Term Consequences of Childhood Sexual Abuse by Gender of Victim." *American Journal of Preventative Medicine* 28, no. 5 (2005): 430–38, www.researchgate.net/publication/7847543_Long-Term_Consequences_of_Childhood_Sexual_Abuse_by_Gender_of_Victim.

Sinozich, Sofi, and Lynn Langton. "Rape and Sexual Assault Victimization Among College Age Females 1995–2013." US Department of Justice, Bureau of Justice Statistics, Office of Justice Programs (December 2014): 1, 3, 4, www.bjs.gov/content/pub/pdf/rsavcaf9513.pdf.

Truman, Jennifer L., and Rachel E. Morgan. "Criminal Victimization, 2015." US Department of Justice, Bureau of Justice Statistics, Office of Justice Programs (October 2016): 6, www.bjs.gov/content/pub/pdf/cv15.pdf.

Works Cited: Words and Terms

BJS: Bureau of Justice Statistics, US Department of Justice, "Rape and Sexual Assault: Terms and Definitions." Last modified June 27, 2017, www.bjs.gov/index.cfm?ty=tp&tid=317#terms_def.

CAPTA: *The Child Abuse Prevention and Treatment Act.* Washington, DC: Children's Bureau, US Department of Health and Human Services, Administration for Children and Families, Administration on Children, Youth and Families, 2010: 31, www.acf.hhs.gov/sites/default/files/cb/capta2010.pdf.

CDC: Basile, Kathleen C., et al. *Sexual Violence Surveillance: Uniform Definitions and Recommended Data Elements.* Atlanta: Centers for Disease Control and Prevention, 2014: 11, 13, 15, 16, www.cdc.gov/violenceprevention/pdf/sv_surveillance_definitionsl-2009-a.pdf.

DSM-5: *Diagnostic and Statistical Manual of Mental Disorders: DSM-5.* 5th ed. Arlington, VA: American Psychiatric Association, 2013: 123, 155, 271, 339, 483, 663.

Additional Copyright information

Your Voice© by Ella Andrews
Letter to the Deacon© by Dina Black
Woman-Up© by Imani Capri
Saturdays© by Jennifer Carmer-Hall
I Want to Stay Alive© by Joan Clare
Reclamation© Jane Cochrane
Pinball© by G. Donald Cribbs
Dear Diary© Maya Demri
Where I Go When I Go Away© by Aaluk Edwardson
In A Series of Silences© by Sharon Abra Hanen
Language of Dance© by Janet Goldblatt Holmes
Hummingbird Hearts© by Carrie Jones
Pearls of Wisdom© by Laura H. Kelly
I Know© by Aster Lee
Sleep Well© by Allison Maloney
Things I Haven't Said© by Melissa Marr
Finding What's Good© by Bryson McCrone
Never Stop Rebelling© by Barbara McLean
The Interrogation Room© by Stephanie Oakes
Little Girls© by Larena Patrick
The Letter I Never Sent© by Shanyn Kay Sprague
Doll House© by Misha Kamau James Tyler
A Word© by Susan Vaught
First Memory© by Linda D. Wattley
Heart© by Carol Lynch Williams